P9-CQN-383

Also by John D. Husband

Maggie Again
a novel

Single Over Thirty

single over thirty

witty insights into the single life

(now that you're not a kid anymore)

JOHN D. HUSBAND

Talywain Press

Talywain Press

Publisher's Cataloging-in-Publication
(Provided by Quality Books, Inc.)

Husband, John D.
Single Over Thirty : witty insights into the single life now that you're not a kid anymore / John D. Husband.
p. cm.
LCCN 2003095203
ISBN 0-9741942-7-1

1. Single people. 2. Middle aged persons. 3. Dating (Social customs) 4. Mate selection. I. Title.

HQ800.H78 2004 305.9'0652
QBI03-200690

BVG 01

For Margaret
Johnny
Susan &
Jimmy

Contents

Introduction

According to the U.S. Census Bureau, there are 288 million people in the United States, 160 million of whom are over the age of 30. And 30 percent of those are single. Ergo, there are 48 million single people over 30 milling about in the United States alone. Lord knows how many worldwide.

This book is for all of them.

Single Over Thirty is about real singles -- the people you and I know. The singles who don't chug-a-lug their beer or groove on wet tee-shirt contests. Most of them have never seen the inside of a singles bar. If they have children, our singles tend to be good fathers and mothers. They lead stable lives, shoulder responsibilities, and take care of themselves and their friends.

In short, Single Over Thirty is about singles as most of them really are.

These columns were written in once-a-month installments since November 1993. They began as a monthly update by the then-coordinator of Three Plus, an off-shoot of New Beginnings, the 1,400-member self-help group for divorced and separated people in the Washington DC area. When the Three-Plus coordinator (me) ran out of house-keeping comments for the newsletter, I started writing light hearted commentaries about the stuff real single lives are made of. Two years later, my successor agreed to take over as coordinator only if I would save him from the drudgery of writing the column. We changed the column's name to "etcetera," then a few years later when it went onto the Internet, it became "Single Over Thirty." And through the magic of cyberspace, its readership broadened far beyond New Beginnings to include readers throughout the United States and Canada, Norway, Japan, Germany, the United Kingdom, Australia, and beyond.

You may notice as you read these columns the mention of meetings. Usually, they are New Beginnings meetings consisting of 14 to 20 participants, a host/hostess and a facilitator who discuss topics of interest to people making the adjustment from married life to single life.

You may also notice that some of the columns do not apply exclusively to singles. Sorry about that, but some singles issues are just not exclusively ours.

And, while I'm making advanced apologies, I'd like to apologize for my male point of view. I've tried to be as balanced as possible but, alas, I'm a man. And there are some things about women -- like shopping, libido, and style -- that I just don't have a handle on. And I know it sometimes shows.

Finally, I'd like to thank the people who have subscribed to my column on the Internet. Their feedback has helped keep the column honest, relevant and on track. I am very grateful to them.

-- John D. Husband
January 2006

Humor is also a way of saying something serious.

-- T.S. Eliot

*The Alien View * Couplers * Great Dates * Kissing * The Sustinance of Friends * Of Pots and Modules * Ready * Six Steps * Water Walking* Dry Dock * Negotiables*

The Alien View

Can you imagine how we would look to visiting aliens? They would think we were crazy.

They'd see single men and women, most of whom are unhappy to some degree with their lack of coupledness. The men want women. And the women want men. And there are lots of men and lots of women. They crowd dance floors together — scores of them (us) packed in together in darkened gymnasiums. They travel miles to picnics and discussions and wine tastings and parties. They swarm to beaches and singles bars and concerts and crabfests. But they don't get together. Sometimes when they're in discussion groups together, they lament their singleness, tell woeful tales of unrequited attempts at togetherness, decry the character flaws of their former other halves. It breaks your heart to hear some of their stories.

Seeing all this, an alien would be dumbfounded. Why suffer when the solution seems so obvious? Get together. Just do it. Quit your belly aching. Get out there and couple. If he spoke English and didn't get green ooze all over everything he touched, an alien would probably grab people at random and say, "Here, you go with him and you go with her."

Of course, it wouldn't work. People would separate as quickly as they were united because earthlings have to be turned on first. And aliens have no concept of what it takes to turn someone on. Actually, I'm not so sure myself.

It probably has something to do with the person you used to be married to. That's what you don't want. Or else it's what you do want but you can't find it. Or maybe you figure you made one big mistake and you don't want to make another, so you're cautious. Or perhaps you feel too vulnerable and don't want to get dumped. Again.

Another thing that would baffle aliens is our reluctance to connect with opposite sex people of divergent age, education, ethnicity, race, religion, occupation, political views, and Myers-Briggs scores. Except sometimes.

And then there's the preference thing — which is the biggest conundrum of them all. Physical attraction between the sexes is an emotional thing. Sometimes sparks fly and sometimes they don't. And no one seems to fully understand why or why not.

It's all very complicated. We could never get aliens to understand — even if we had the words to explain it to them. No wonder there are so few sightings of aliens. They're probably avoiding us.

Couplers

There are people in this world who are always part of a couple. It starts, I suspect, some time shortly after puberty. I can see it now: "This is Jacob. He's 13. And this is Jacob's little girlfriend, Penelope." (Titters all around.) They're so cute.

By high school, Penelope, of course, is history. But Jacob has a new girl friend who was always at his side. Her parents joke that Jacob spends more time at their house than at his own. The young couple broke up during the summer before his senior year. But by the time school started again, Jacob was a couple with someone else. He had a new girlfriend in junior college and another one when he transferred to State. He married young and divorced after a time, moving right into another relationship. And another.

It's all a mystery to me. Is he just very skilled at developing relationships? Or is he perhaps very needy? Or very wise about women?

When I was in high school, I didn't have a girlfriend - certainly not one that was with me at all times. Nor when I was in college. I flirted with some, drooled from afar over others, and became pals with still others. But I never really had a clinging girlfriend grafted to my elbow.

Don't get me wrong. Relationships can be wonderful. But my experience has been that it takes time to develop them. Then they last for a long time, sometimes forever. And if they end, one usually goes through a lengthy recovery period before being ready for a new one. Then the long getting-to-know-each-other process starts all over again.

Not so with couplers.

Couplers seem to be programmed by some mysterious imperative that craves the symmetry of couplehood. When they are alone, which isn't very often, they look and act like everyone else. But when they're together, wham, they connect, they couple, they are as one.

Well, after all these years, I may have stumbled upon a partial insight into the couplers' psyche. I was at a meeting that began innocently enough discussing how men feel about being called for a date by a woman they don't know well. I said I didn't get all that many calls. And when I did, it was often from someone I would not have asked out, resulting either in a dead-end date or a stammering, excuse-making, inept and embarrassing declination.

And then it happened. A man whose approach is the opposite of mine spoke. He liked being called. He loved going out with the callers. He went steady with one for a year and a half, another for eight months, and a third for nearly three years. He had been coupled all through high school, all through college and, when he was married, he and his wife were inseparable. He was at the meeting because he had just broken off a relationship and had not yet begun a new one. This was incredibly good luck. Couplers are seldom available for discussions because they're occupied by their coupling activities. This guy was a rare find; a small window of opportunity just begging to be examined. I wanted to take him back to the lab and study him.

Because he's not like me, I was tempted to be critical of him. But I found myself admiring him instead. I was sure he had some very special skills.

Maybe he just commits easily, a rare and highly valued quality in a man. Maybe he views women as interchangeable - like modules. One fits as well as another. Maybe he's just a very nice guy who women like immediately. Or perhaps he's just doing what comes naturally.

At first, I was disappointed that he didn't impart much information. He seemed to have very little relationship savvy. I wondered why. Then it hit me. He has ended as many relationships as he's started. Ah, there's the down side. Perhaps, the more relationships one has had, the less one knows about them. Think about it. In order to start a continuing series of relationships, one has to have ended an equal number. And that suggests one can't sustain a relationship. They're probably the last people one should look to for enlightenment.

That meeting was nearly a year ago. He and his new girlfriend (big surprise) have since started a business together.

They're inseparable.

Great Dates

Now that you and that new certain somebody have already had dinner twice and seen three movies, it's time for a change, some variety, some imaginative places to go and things to do. Here are some great date ideas collected from all over the place — including from readers like you.

A short trip away:

1. Spend a day at the races. Whether it's horse races, demolition derbies, dog races, or The Celebrated Jumping Frog of Calaveras County, there's got to be one near you. The less you know about racing sports, the more of an adventure it can be.

2. Take art supplies to a beach, lake or other picturesque spot and draw or paint side by side.

3. Go to the airport or mall and people watch.

4. Do a food court date where you sample from every little food place, making a full meal. Bring your own doggy bag.

5. Go to a craft fair and actually buy something unique.

6. Tour a winery, take samples and bring a few bottles home.

7. Find a secluded place and have a photo shoot. Take pictures of each other. You can enjoy them an hour later — even sooner if you have a digital camera.

8. Have a video game war at the nearest arcade. ...And don't be intimidated by the skills of those kids who have been hanging around the arcade since they were infants.

9. Go to an amusement park and try to win something for each other on the midway.

10. Go to a high school play, a community band concert, an art show, a house tour, an air show, visit a marina, or join in whatever else your local newspaper says is happening in your town.

11. Wander leisurely through a public garden.

12. Explore the zoo.

Weather and geography permitting:

1. Build a snowman, snow sculpture, or ice castle.

2. Get two rain-ponchos so you can take a walk in the rain. Splash in every puddle. Get wet. Be fearless. (But have dry clothes and a cup of hot cocoa waiting at home.)

3. Most of the earth's surface is water. Use some of it. Go fishing or sailing or swimming or scuba diving.

4. The sun is free. Bask in it at the nearest beach or lake front. Bring sun screen.

5. Using just sand and water, create an astounding work of art at the beach.

6. Find some calm water and rent a canoe for two.

Around town:

1. Go bike riding. If available, consider renting a bicycle built for two. Take a picnic with you.

2. Play tennis, badminton or croquet.

3. Explore your town on foot.

4. Go fly a kite. Hobby stores generally have kite kits. Or build one from scratch. Learn how on the Internet.

With others:

1. Invite some friends over for a murder mystery party.

2. Try to draw each other.

3. Have a bulla-bulla hunt — an especially good way to include children. While the person who is "it" leaves the room, the others hide a household item somewhere in the room. The person then returns to search for it while the others in the room sing bulla-bulla, getting louder as the "it" person gets closer, and softer as he/she moves away.

At home for two:

1. Bake a loaf or two of bread. Sit down together and eat a few slices while it's still warm and butter melts on it. Then, while it's still fresh, take a loaf with you as a gift when you visit friends or go to a party.

2. Set up a fish tank.

3. Cook your date his/her favorite meal.

4. Wash and wax one or both of your cars together.

5. Play cards, put together a jigsaw puzzle, solve a crossword, play a board game or just hang out.

Kissing

O**nly seven years separate** the youngest of my four brothers from the oldest. I'm next to the youngest and, as a pre-teen, idolized my next-to-oldest brother, Phil, who was then a card-carrying, hormone-raging, teenager. He told me that my middle brother, Bert, never made a hit with the girls because he never tried to kiss them.

I was appalled. Kissing in the movies was bad enough, but to do it in real life when you weren't married (and therefore required to) was beyond the pale.

In the intervening years, I came to modify my position somewhat. During courtship it was enormous fun and seemed to work rather well. During marriage, it was either perfunctory or preparatory, but it still worked well and was unambiguous. Then came the later single years, otherwise known variously as the second single season, the middle aged adolescent years, and the puerile time-warp. And now kissing is again a mystery. They still do it in the movies and on TV — although now they do it with jaws fully agape. Open drawbridges come to my mind. I try not to think about what else might be happening within the resulting chasm.

In real life, I assume introductory kisses are more modest. Although I haven't done enough research to prove it, I would think first kisses tend to be the old fashioned kind and that the movie/TV open-mouthed sloshes are reserved for those subsequent and more private moments that are none of our business.

It's difficult to predict how a kiss will be received.

When my daughter, in her early 20s, described a date who walked her to her doorstep then hesitated. My daughter thought "Oh no, I hope he isn't going to kiss me. I'd rather siphon gasoline."

And then, by contrast, there was a now-married middle aged couple whose magic moment was the kiss. "Then he bent over and gently kissed me on the mouth. I was swept away," recalls the wistful bride.

I'm not exactly the kissing bandit, but I have attempted a kiss every now and again since I've been single. It may be a big disappointment to you to learn that they have not all worked out well — like the adroit woman who could land my kiss lightly upon her cheek no matter how ardently I was aiming it elsewhere. And the woman with whom, on our fourth date, I had been holding hands, schmoozing and trading compliments all evening. Then I kissed her. She looked at me blankly and said, "What was the purpose of that?"

Why can't kisses be as uncomplicated as hugs? Hugs seem to work so well, so easily. "Are you a hugger?" you ask someone you're not sure of. "How about a nice big hug?" you say to someone you are. There are no hidden messages. You and the hugee are not transported to a new level of intimacy. It's just a hug. It's all so safe, satisfying and predictable.

Why can't a kiss be like that?

The Sustenance of Friends

When you come into this world, you don't know any of its inhabitants. And when you leave it, virtually everyone who was here when you arrived has already left.

So it's up to you to get out there and meet some new people on your own.

You need to make friends - not just acquaintances. Acquaintances you'll make anyway - guaranteed. Just by being in the way, you can make acquaintances. What sets friends apart is that you care about them. And that makes all the difference.

High school is a good place to make life-long friends. In fact, you may still maintain some long-term friends from your teen years. I certainly do. They're a unique part of my personal history, and absolutely irreplaceable.

There are, of course, all sorts of friends who appear and disappear at different stages as one progresses from the cradle to one's present circumstance. But, for our purposes, let's concentrate on singledom and your over-thirtyishness, and how friends impact them.

Where to make friends:

You can make friends practically anywhere - even at the supermarket; or so I've heard. But I don't know how. I've been food shopping a thousand times and I don't recall ever seeing the same customer twice. Once a check-out clerk said, "How y' doin'?" to me and for a minute I thought she remembered me. But then she added "Sir." And I knew she was just following company policy.

Supermarkets and other places where one tends to be invisible can be a challenge. The best places, I'm convinced, are those where you give part of yourself: They include:

(1.) At work, assuming you interface with others. A lighthouse keeper, for instance, might not, but office workers and most others surely would.

(2.) At social events, like dances, parties, picnics, hikes, and any other place one gets out and mixes it up with others in a relaxed atmosphere.

(3.) At school, whether it's an adult education course or you're going for a degree, there's a lot of interfacing with a mix of others with similar interests, be it art, taxidermy, or nuclear physics.

(4.) Volunteering, by which I mean doing anything for the common good for which there is no pay. By simple virtue of their being there in the first place, your fellow volunteers tend to be givers as opposed to takers. And they make the best friends.

How to make friends - the rules:

(1.) Be nice. Validate the people around you. Be upbeat, thoughtful, generous and considerate.

(2.) Listen. Don't do all the talking and, when others are talking, pay attention. You may learn something useful.

(3.) Be responsive. Laugh at jokes. Show appreciation. Give full attention. React.

(4.) Smile. Be generous with your smiles, but smile appropriately. There's a difference between a smile and a relentless grin.

(5.) Keep your promises. Don't make promises you can't keep, but keep those you make. It builds trust.

(6.) Be yourself. The two prime rules about meeting new people are: (a.) unless you have earned at least two Academy Awards, be yourself. If you try to be someone else, you'll be spotted as a phony immediately; and (b.) if having been yourself, they still don't like you, don't take it personally. What do they know? Move on.

How to keep friends:

(1.) Keep doing what you did to make friends in the first place.

Types of friends:

Casual friends. The people whose names you might know, to whom you nod when passing and make small talk when you're together. Under the right circumstances, they could become close friends.

Event friends. Personal example: She finds me and drags me to the dance floor and muscles me through the steps of the El Paso, simultaneously shouting instructions into my ear. I'm a slow learner, but we're nevertheless El Paso buddies. I suppose if I were a quick study, she'd have long-since lost interest. Sometimes, I don't even know she's at the dance until the ominous strains of The El Paso float through the air and she materializes at the end of my arm, pulling me toward the floor. Otherwise, I seldom see her.

Former friends. "Former," suggests you had a falling out and no longer care about each other. Shame on one or both of you.

Future friends. Everybody, potentially.

Wannabe friends. People who relentlessly invite you to things you don't want to go to. And manufacture mutual interests. I had a male friend who was about my height and twice my girth. He thought it would be a cool idea if we had dinner occasionally. So we did. Once. He ate at the speed of light and kept pointing to my food and saying "are you going to eat that?" I told him he was a one-time-only exception to my general practice of only having one-on-one dinners with pretty women, of which he was definitely not one. It was not one of my most tactful moments, but it worked.

Don't wannabe friends. A would-be friend doesn't need to refuse your overtures; they just have to let you do all the friendship's maintenance work. Then when you realize you're in the friendship by yourself, you withdraw. It's a good system when you think about it. No one actually rejects the other. You just sort of drift painlessly apart. It's better than being rejected and a whole lot better than having to endure a blunt and humiliating recitation of his/her reasons -- which probably aren't the real reason anyway.

Wanna NOT be friends. This category is populated by people who steal, take drugs, inflict pain, bore you, stink, lie, cheat, infect, lose control or take two parking spaces at the shopping center. Avoid them. They'll cause you heartache and grief.

18. - Single Over Thirty

Best friend (singular). Not a good idea, in my view. It can be distancing and suggests cliquishness. For men, it's not really an issue. If they have a best friend (other than their significant others) they seldom refer to them as such. But many grown women do. A "best friend" was fine when they were prepubescent and shared secrets, sleep-overs and tea parties. But grown women should elevate all their valued friends to "best friend" status. Having an adult "best friend" is like having one favorite child at the expense of your other children.

Sexy friends. Marry one of these critters - or at least enter into a lengthy relationship. These are keepers. But make sure they are really friends and not just irresistibly sexy.

Of Pots and Modules

Partners are like computer modules, a woman friend once told me. You simply remove the defective one and replace it with one that works — like changing a light bulb.

That may sound rather cold and bloodless. But I don't think that's what she intended. She was simply poo-pooing the opposite notion — the notion that there's just one lid for every pot — just one.

For my part, I'd like the pot analogy to be the right one. I'd like to think that there's someone out there for everyone — even divorced people — and that fate moves one inexorably toward that person — like "Sleepless in Seattle" or "The Bridges of Madison County." ...Or any of the syrupy movies that were made when I was a kid.

Unfortunately, that has not been my experience. I know some very difficult pots on whom no lid could fit. And wonderful lids who have the good-will and adaptability to fit virtually any pot they choose. I have also found that, most of the time, fate seems pretty indifferent to the whole process; content to sit back, fold its arms, and let things not happen.

20. - Single Over Thirty

To carry the module analogy to a ridiculous extreme, one must be sure it was the module that was defective before one can successfully find a suitable replacement. And, whereas there may be many appropriate replacements, there are myriad inappropriate ones. And finding the former while avoiding the latter is no mean task.

One more positive thought about modules: If we all thought of coupling in the module sense, and not in the "there's one special person out there for me" pot sense, break-ups would be a lot easier. Instead of agonizing over the loss of the unique, the irreplaceable, the pre-ordained one, we could shrug it off as a bad fit and get on with our lives.

Ready

When my former beach house buddy insisted he wasn't ready for a relationship with the marvelous woman he was dating, I laughed at his foolishness.

He's the most steady, enlightened, ready man I know and I told him so. So to make his point, he listed for me all the reasons he's not ready. He was very convincing. And when he was done, I had to agree with him. He's not ready. Nobody's ready. Probably no one ever has been. Ever.

If being ready is the criterion, Adam and Eve should have remained "just friends." As a couple, they were a disaster. They had no relationship skills, no prior experience, and I hear Eve was jealous — although I'm not sure of whom. Anyway, the results were predictable: First there was that nasty business about the apple; then they raised a son who committed the world's first homicide.

Napoleon was away with the troops for months, years at a time. No quick jetting home on a weekend pass. No furloughs. No R&R. Yet he and Josephine managed one of history's best known romances.

And how about Romeo and Juliet? How could they be

ready? They were just kids.

So much for biblical, historical, and fictional relationship readiness.

In today's world, as in the past, being altogether ready is a pipe dream. Ready for what? What exactly does a "ready" person do that the rest of us don't? Do they have no preference in such fundamental domestic matters as loading the dishwasher, hanging the toilet paper correctly, or squeezing the toothpaste tube from the end forward? Are they never testy, tired or tactless? Do they carry no baggage? Harbor no resentments? Favor no vices? Are they endlessly fair? Consummately kind? Perpetually perky?

I've never met a "ready" person but if they're that relentlessly perfect, I don't think I'd be very comfortable around them. Granted, some people are more ready than others. And being more ready is better than being less ready. But nobody's totally ready. This whole relationship thing is a bit of a crap shoot for which there is no fool-proof preparation. You get no guarantees up front. It's sort of a grand, scary adventure — like Butch Cassidy and the Sundance Kid when they jumped off the cliff and into the mountain stream waaay down below to evade the Pinkerton posse.

If my friend had been Sundance, he'd have wanted to sign up for swimming lessons at the YMCA first.

Six Steps

If you are destined to becoming half of a loving couple, you can expect to pass through these six all-important steps, according to a source I've long since forgotten:

Step #1. *Awareness* — You notice the other person.

Step #2. *Acceptance* — You nod hello, perhaps memorize his/her name now. Maybe later. There's plenty of time.

Step #3. *Caring* — The other takes on some importance to you. You like them. You probably think they're sexy. You want to know them better. If you haven't already memorized the other's name, this is a good time. Things will go easier for you.

Step #4. *Trust* — You judge the other person to be safe, comfortable. You are confident you can reveal yourself without being invalidated or used. You're not a couple yet, but hang in there, you're getting close.

Step #5. *Affirmation* — You demonstrate to each other that the caring and trust are mutual. You probably both utter those fateful three little words. There's no turning back.

Step #6. *Celebration* — Together, you do something about it. Dinner by candle light. Marriage. Something like that.

That list is like a TV quiz show. The steps get more difficult as the potential rewards get bigger. Anybody can pick an interesting face out of a crowd or nod hello. Caring is only slightly more difficult — especially if the other person is (in your view) sexy. Trust can be slow; affirmation, risky; and celebration, downright scary.

Let's test the list using two strangers who belong to the same political party:

They first see each other at a fund raiser. He notices she's pretty. She notices that he notices. He says hello. She nods and smiles. He smiles back.

Time out. We're already out of sequence. She's not supposed to be pretty (ergo sexy) until step three. Never mind. Through cunning and deception, they find a way to be working on arranging flyers by zip code so they'll qualify for third class. (The flyers, that is. We're assuming the couple is already first class.) When they're done, after making small talk, he asks her if she's free for supper. She is.

Okay, now they are solidly into step three, caring. On to trust. A lot of conversation, demonstrated character traits, thoughtfulness and attention ought to take care of that. And that doesn't happen over one order of London broil with bearnaise sauce. A good deal of talk about politics passes between them. Promises are kept. They laugh a lot. Disagreements never turn toxic. This is not an overt test period. For them, trust is more of a subconscious thing that blossoms on its own. No yellow flags pop up. Mutual trust develops slowly and naturally until...

One of them says almost casually to the other, "I love you." And the other responds simply, "Me too." Then adds something awkward like, "I don't mean I love me too, I mean I love you. Boy, do I ever?" They both laugh and embrace and I prefer not to describe the scene further. The important thing is that they have spontaneously aced Step #5, affirmation.

Assuming they maintain their resolve, Step #6 should be easy. It won't be, of course. Two separate, independent, unrelated people have just decided to squeeze their lives into the same space. But if anyone can do it they can. It certainly ought to be a distinct possibility for any couple who breezed through the first five steps so famously.

Or at all.

Water-Walking

"**When I first met him,** I thought he could walk on water," a woman said at a recent meeting.

"Me too." chimed in a chorus of nodding heads.

"Then I got to see who he really was."

"Oh yes, yes. The scum." said the chorus.

"We settled in to a period of borderline tolerance, boredom, irritation and finally, pfftt, we ended it."

Responding to this common relationship experience, some people in the room nodded their heads so vigorously I wouldn't have been surprised to see one clear the shoulders entirely and roll across the floor.

When such an extreme consensus invades a discussion, I'm never sure what to do. I usually mention such has not been my experience — which is a lot like disagreeing. And that makes them more adamant.

In truth, I don't know anyone I worship that much. I never met a man who could walk on water or a woman who belonged on a pedestal — even when I was most smitten.

The whole phenomenon seems unreal to me. I don't mind worship. It might be nice to have someone think you are that incredible. It's the part that comes afterwards that frazzles me — the part where she gets to know who he really is and he becomes intolerable, boring, irritating and, finally, history.

I can't prove it, but my guess is that the guy is no more intolerable than he is a water-walker. His real character traits are probably never recognized at all. From the start he was an invention. What's more, he gets to be invented twice; once as a water-walker and then as a rascal. The unfair part is that the inventee only gets to be a water-walker for a short time — until the inventor can no longer sustain the water-walker illusion — then he gets to be a villain.

And in her memory, he remains a villain for the rest of time.

Dry Dock

So you're getting ready for a dinner date that has some real potential. This could be special. The sheer anticipation puts you in a mellow mood. So instead of taking the requisite shower, you decide to luxuriate in the bath tub.

Big mistake.

That thing is either for decoration, or for washing small children and household pets. You're not suppose to take a bath in it. You don't fit. You haven't fit since the fourth grade. The average bathtub is made for people who are four feet long and seven inches thick. Otherwise, you can't get your major self under water. You're not really taking a bath, you're just washing yourself while sitting on a wet spot. It's ludicrous. Like skiing on a snow cone.

But you already know all that. So why did you buy such a small tub? It came with the house, right? In fact, small bathtubs with attached showers (in case you want to get clean) come with virtually every house.

Granted, there are big tubs. I know, I've seen them in the movies, on TV, and in soap ads. They're big enough that the model to sit comfortably (and modestly) in a sea of suds. And some people actually own big tubs and Jacuzzis and such. But overwhelmingly, bathtubs are small. Too small.

Who decides the size? Certainly not the bather. Or even the one who buys the house. Or sells the house. Or builds the house. It may be decided by the person who designs the house. But more likely it's the one who employs the designer; a bottom-line kind of a guy who reasons something like this: "A small tub makes the bathroom look bigger and conserves water. No one ever uses it anyway. It's just there to keep shower water off the bathroom floor. But it's a bathroom so you have to install a bathtub. If you don't, the sales brochures will call it a half bath and the value will plummet."

And that's why your chest, your stomach and your legs below the knee remain in dry dock while the rest of you rationalizes that you're taking a bath.

My renewed focus on the minusculity of modern bathtubs came about when I found a page from a sort of diary I kept when I was 12 years old. The entry for January 4th was "I took another bath today. I rode my bicycle." Those days of large tubs and a small me put me in mind of baths and how, from that day forward, tubs have become increasingly cramped.

In every bathroom in every house I've ever lived in as an adult — every home in which I've been a guest, every hotel and motel and guest quarters I've ever stayed at, the bathtubs have been too darned small.

Negotiables

A **soon-to-be-married** friend told me she had learned during her singledom that, in relationships, everything is negotiable. I liked that view. It seemed to work for her. I adopted it as my own view.

Then I started going to discussion meetings with other divorced people and was vaguely disturbed to find people listing the most incredible non-negotiables. Men who don't share their feelings. Overweight women. Men who don't respect a woman's independence. Women who expect the man to pay for everything. Soon I recognized a pattern. People were listing the characteristics that caused conflict in their marriages.

My problem with that criteria is that it represents such a small slice of all the things that can wreak havoc in a relationship.

I have no quarrel with anyone who doesn't want to repeat the old miseries. What I do resist, however, is the creation of a steel vault in one's mind that contains stuff one won't negotiate. Negotiate doesn't mean accept. One can negotiate and ultimately reject. It's like the old saw professing that all prayers are answered — but sometimes the answer is no.

For a time, I thought I had no non-negotiables. But someone asked me if there were any circumstances in which I would date a serial killer, someone with a highly contagious terminal disease, or a woman who had totally lost touch with reality. I had to admit that the first two always had been non-negotiables and the third is now.

Nevertheless, it seems to me prudent to exercise some restraint in one's choice of non-negotiables. Here's a bit of fiction to make my point:

What if late in the 1990s, a few days after he had been named People Magazine's "The Best Looking Man in the World", Brad Pitt was in town testifying before The House Environmental Affairs subcommittee on his pet cause, the depletion of the ozone layer? And what if House staffer Anna Maria Hyde helped him organize his testimony and critiqued it. When his testimony was complete, he might have asked her to recommend a place for dinner — and to join him. And she probably would have suggested Toscanini's. They very likely would have dined on Roast Peking Duck with white wine sauce and topped the meal off with a couple of flaming Brandy Alexanders. Anna Maria is a very pretty, charming, bright woman, so Pitt would certainly have wanted to see her again. If he had to spend a few days in New York but would be back on the weekend, for instance, he couldn't help wondering out loud if Anna Maria could show him the rest of Washington. She of course would have declined because, when the meal was over, he would have lit up one of Anna Maria's non-negotiables: a cigarette..

So Anna Maria would go back to her boring old apartment and Brad Pitt would ultimately quit smoking and marry Jennifer Aniston.

I hope your reaction to that story is something like "Couldn't Anna Maria at least have talked to him about it?"

But talking about it is another term for negotiating. And Anna Maria has her principles. ...And her non-negotiables.

Remember, this story is fiction. For all I know, Brad Pitt never smoked and would have still married Jennifer even if Anna Maria had been real. And less rigid.

Wobbly Arrows

*Cupid * Smitten * In It By Yourself * Late Again * Storm Warnings * Rejection * Priorities * Glue * Rituals*

Cupid

This may be a bit of a stretch, but let's say you are Cupid and you can't find your quiver full of arrows.

Now you must wing it, so to speak, because even without arrows, you still are duty-bound to enamor two perfect strangers to such a degree that they'll act goofy and want to grow old together; two strangers whose life experiences have been poles apart. One lived life as a man, the other as a woman. And you, Cupid, having read "Men Are From Mars, Women Are From Venus" know exactly how different that can be.

Your mission: Get the male stranger to bring flowers to the female stranger and get her to sew a button onto his suit. Both must do so voluntarily and unbidden. She can't ask him to bring flowers; he can't ask her to sew. This is a formidable task. But you can do it. You're Cupid. Who needs arrows?

Based on your experience in real life, how would you make it happen? What does he say and what does she say, if anything, that produces the magic moment? Or is it a glance? Timing? Commonality? Or pure and simple hormones?

38. - Single Over Thirty

To test your arrow-less expertise, you appear at a local singles bar. You will a man who is standing around to walk up to a woman who is seated and say "Can I buy you a drink?" Nah, that's so obvious. Not worthy of a Roman god, albeit a small, chubby, invisible one.

You opt, instead, to appear at a singles dance. You will him to ask her to dance. He does, several times during the evening. He asks her if she minds if he calls. She doesn't so he does. After a bit of phone chatter, he asks her for a dinner date — a weekday to start, so it won't last long in case they don't hit it off. As it happens, they *do* hit it off, so he asks her if she'd like to do something on a weekend, like go to a play or the county fair or a craft show. She would.

They laugh a lot and tell each other their stories — where they grew up, siblings, and what their hobbies are. Nothing very personal yet. No stories of unrequited love. No admission of real weaknesses or errors or regrets. They keep it light.

They touch a lot and make rather flattering observations about each other. "You have an incredible memory. You take care of yourself. You have good taste in clothes — that's a nice combination. You poured coffee from one cup to another exceptionally well without spilling a drop." They talk about similar interests and tastes and opinions. They hold hands and kiss, tentatively at first. They talk. And talk. And surprise each other with little thoughtfulnesses.

Now they're on their way. They care. Falling in love is a slam dunk. You, Cupid, did well without firing a single arrow. You withdraw. There are other worlds to conquer.

What if neither of them dances and they don't go to bars? What if they are, for instance, country folks, both helping a mutual neighbor with the haying? A full wagon has just left for the barn and an empty one is in sight, but not here yet. So they have a few minutes. She sits in the shade of a huckleberry bush and pops little blue berries into her mouth. He thinks she looks fetching, beads of sweat dribbling down her rosy cheeks; hay chaff clinging to unruly strands of her sun-bleached hair; dark, moist crescents under the arms of her oversized shirt.

Who could resist?

He globs onto the berries — his pretend reason for sticking around — and observes aloud that the little bit of a breeze that sweeps across the field is a welcome relief. She agrees. He asks her name and where she's from. She tells him and he volunteers the same about himself. Oh-oh, the second hay wagon is here.

Later, they chat again atop the final hay wagon headed for the barn. An authentic hay ride — practically their first date. He tries to find out when she might be haying again, or if she goes to meetings at the Grange Hall, or church, or the strawberry socials in the village. And if all that fails, just as the wagon is pulling into the barn, he asks her if she has a phone and if she minds if he calls her. If she screws up her face and asks "why?" it's all over. Otherwise, you little mythological butterball, you're batting two for two.

Okay, now you go back to the bar. You've avoided it as long as you could, but huge gobs of couples are smitten there. You don't know exactly why. Maybe it's the liquor. Maybe it's those little arrows you have been flinging around so indiscriminately — before you misplaced them. You spot a perfectly fine man wandering about the place — obviously on the prowl. You will him to ask some woman he doesn't know if he can buy her a drink. She gives him a quick glance, shifts in her seat so her back is more squarely toward him, and goes on talking to her girlfriend.

He asks another. "Do I know you?" she asks icily, then moves to another seat.

Three's the charm. He tries again. This one rolls her eyes and complains to the bar tender that he's bothering her.

She is followed by a woman who tells him he's drunk, one who suggests he gets lost, one who responds with "and what might you be expecting in return?" and hysterical laughter from a woman who never actually answered his question.

Then finally, finally, the woman seated next to him at the bar initiates a conversation. "You're sitting in my boyfriend's seat," she says.

And you, Cupid, armed with a new appreciation for the power of your little bow and arrow, leave the bar and return to your little apartment to look one more time for your misplaced quiver.

Smitten

It was such a sweet, gentle discussion meeting until the very end.

That was when the professional therapist in charge summed up saying, essentially, that finding a partner (as he did, thank you) pretty much depends upon one's willingness to ignore physical attraction and look for compatible people with depth of character.

I said, "Whoa. They're both important. In fact, the first attraction is generally physical for me. I don't find out about character depth until later."

I doubt if anyone heard me totally. I could hardly hear myself, for I had pushed THE BUTTON. Several rather dowdy women went off like air raid sirens, proclaiming my view to be shallow and invalid. One even suggested my life would be a lot better if I looked at women's character first.

Think about that for a moment. I walk into a crowded room and look about for women of depth and character. How do I identify them? Can I safely assume that those who attract me by their appearance would not interest me once I got to know them? And that those to whom I was not attracted would?

42. - Single Over Thirty

Or look at it from a woman's viewpoint. She has a choice of two new men, one handsome, the other a toad. She will get to know them — for better or worse — as she spends time with them. Does she go with the toad? I don't think so.

Terry Gorski, in his celebrated relationships tape, says if you see someone across a crowded room who is immediately attractive to you, "turn around and walk the other way."

I disagree with him too.

My understanding of the phenomenon of romantic attraction is that, through an incredibly complex and personalized process that begins even before puberty, one develops some very individualized preferences, both physically and personality-wise. Sometimes either the physical preference or the personality preference misfires, in which case some remedial therapy may be in order. Or perhaps one just needs to get out and meet some new people. But most of the time, it works. We non-professionals call the result being "smitten."

The confusion comes in when someone follows his physical preferences only to find the person who turned him on is otherwise a mismatch. And from that he may wrongly reason that he should not pursue opposite sex people who turn him on because he can't get along with them. To assume so is a prime example of deriving more information from an experience than is really there. And Mark Twain agrees with me; that was the whole point of his quip: "A cat that once sits on a hot stove will never again sit on a hot stove, but he won't sit on a cold one either."

If he was right, it ought to follow that, having once been burned by a very attractive poor choice, one should not automatically reject all potential love interests one finds alluring.

Most people would agree that nice people come in all sizes and shapes — including those one finds sexy.

...Which brings me to Patty FitzGerald who sat in front of me in Mrs. Yenchar's fifth grade class. Patty was pretty, clean, smart and stuck-up — all the attributes most admired by an 11-year-old boy. She sent me a Valentine card that said, "Birds of a feather flock together. So how about you and me?" I later found she sent the same card to everyone in our class — even the girls. But it was too late to turn back now. I was smitten. Another kid and I even got into an impromptu pushing bout over Patty in the school yard during recess. Patty didn't much care for either of us. She didn't show up for the fight. She didn't care who won. What fifth grader could resist a girl like that?

I liked Patty because she was pretty. I didn't care if she was nice. (She wasn't — not to me, anyway.) I was new at this game and taking it one step at a time. All these years later, of course, I have come to fully appreciate the importance of character and compatibility in choosing a partner.

And that makes me wonder: If I had it all to do over again and could magically go back to being a fifth grader with the knowledge and understanding I have today, would I still have been smitten by Patty FitzGerald?

The answer is almost certainly, "Yes, I would." But I'd have lost interest sooner, and I'd have skipped that school-yard pushing bout altogether.

In It By Yourself

At a party, have you ever talked to someone thinking they were still at your elbow — only to discover they weren't and you had been talking loudly to yourself in a room full of increasingly wary strangers?

Me neither. But it's a scenario that's easy to imagine. And it serves well to demonstrate how devastating it can be when you think the other half of the couple is participating fully in the relationship with you. Then you realize, they aren't; that you are in it all by yourself. All alone. Most of it is happening only in your mind and imagination. The other person is not totally there. They never were. They don't want to be. They don't even want to think about it. Their thoughts are occupied by a different agenda.

More than a decade ago, a woman friend told me about her then ex-boyfriend who had agonized for more than a year over the prospect of marriage. He finally decided yes and asked her. She agreed and he never mentioned it again.

"I was in it all by myself," she told me.

That was the first time I had ever heard the expression. And it brought a lot into focus for me. The fear that one might be in it by oneself can be as spooky as anything else that can go wrong in a relationship.

How do you know if the other person is of the same mind you are? If you ask, they'll probably say something like, "It depends. Of what mind are you?" Now, ready or not, you have to declare it all off the top of your head with no inkling of what kind of response you might get. For me, that would take incredible pluck.

My guess is that the answer comes from your partner in little pieces, now and again, and that you have to avoid getting so enamored by your own romantic visions that you fail to hear what the other person is saying (or not saying.)

Getting back to the theoretical party where you talked-on to someone who had left: There may be a lesson here. If you looked at the person at your elbow as you talked, you certainly would have noticed when he or she left. Or maybe, sensing your genuine interest they would have stuck around.

Whatever the case, you wouldn't have been in it all by yourself.

Late Again

I love the growing practice of a 30-minute flex period before meetings.

Not only is it a great time to schmooze with old friends, sample the refreshments, and then slide gracefully into the meeting, it also acts as a buffer for those of us who have a hard time being anywhere at a precise time.

In the best of all worlds, I would like to be forever prompt — always where I said I'd be at the precise time I said I would. But there's a danger in that sort of obsessive punctuality; the danger that I would some day inadvertently be early. And that would be unconscionable.

Being early is infinitely worse than being late. It wreaks havoc with one's host or hostess who, being used to people being on time or late, is still in the shower, or sitting on the edge of the bed clipping their toe nails, or half dressed and looking for the other shoe, or scrubbing the guest bathroom sink, or finishing the snack that's substituting for supper, or rinsing the dust from the wine goblets. At such a time, only an unspeakable cad would ring the doorbell early.

In the absence of anyone else having delineated the rules of behavior for lateness, I would like to suggest the following:

Barely late: When one is just a few minutes past the agreed-upon hour, one never mentions his or her lateness and acts confident and self-righteous. Nonchalance is powerful stuff. So don't be surprised if your host is so convinced of your promptness that he calls the phone company to get the right time — and then doesn't believe what they tell him.

A little late: We're talking about anywhere from seven to 15 minutes late. One says simply, "Sorry to hold you up. Have you been waiting long?" Then one never mentions it again.

Very late: Shame on you. Apologize. Accept responsibility for egregiously poor planning and make sure it doesn't happen again.

Exceptions to the rule:

Early is acceptable (and being even a little bit late is not) when you are meeting someone at an inhospitable site, in bad weather, after dark.

Late is acceptable when you are attending certain kinds of social events. If you have not committed yourself to an arrival time and no one is inconvenienced by your tardiness, you can arrive with impunity as late as you wish.

Then there are the times when you arrange your time well, you want to be on time, and it's important to be on time, but you're still late because you had to work late, the Cherry Blossom Festival parade blocked your path, or your car conked out.

At such times, when you are greeted at the door with "Oh John, you're always late." Explain the situation with something like, "Oh shut up, Elizabeth."

Storm Warnings

Listening doesn't come easy for me — especially if I think I already know what the person is going to say.

And I've attended enough meetings to know that I'm not alone in that shortcoming. In fact, I may have been the only one listening at a meeting a while ago when one of those people who seldom speaks spoke. He had some advice for us:

"Don't wait for people's actions (to find out what mischief they're capable of), listen to their words. Chances are they'll tell you in advance who they really are and what they're going to do."

That was what he said. But what the group heard was the old saw: "Talk is cheap. Pay no attention to what people say, just watch what they do. Actions speak louder than words."

Everyone agreed with him because they thought he had regurgitated one of those ancient platitudes that make rooms full of people nod their heads in mechanical assent.

Fortunately, he didn't drop the subject. If someone says, for instance, "Oh I'm so undependable," you should believe him, not dismiss the remark as charmingly modest and self-effacing. If a woman describes herself as a free spirit, don't be crest-fallen to find she is still out playing when you stop by for your Saturday date. Because you want to believe the best, you may be thinking of a free spirit as some sweet, irrepressible Holly Golightly. But what she has really told you is that she's egregiously irresponsible; that you are pretty low on her priorities list; that the moment — any moment — is more important than you are. She'll cause you pain. And she told you so up front.

Discussions among single people can — and do — so easily digress into complaints about what former spouses or lovers have done — how righteous we are and how we've nevertheless suffered at the hands of those unscrupulous people we foolishly trusted.

Then along comes this guy who, instead of adding to the litany, tells us we can save ourselves grief by listening, really listening.

And we almost didn't hear him.

Rejection

There I was sitting in the jury box trying to look fair and impartial and praying that this trial would be over this day because I was paying someone to substitute for me at work.

The judge told the plaintiff's table they could reject a few jurors perfunctorily, that is without having to give a reason. They huddled, then the plaintiff's attorney looked up and said, "We excuse John Husband."

I was mortified. "Hey, what're you pickin' on me for," I didn't say, not adding, "I'm very fair and impartial."

Instead I got up and walked out, stopping at the jury office to pick up my $15 check for being a good citizen for a day.

Probably I was rejected because I was clean-shaven and wearing a tie — like some straight arrow who might automatically side with the cops — one of whom the plaintiff was accused of slugging. A gray sweat shirt, a sneer, and a day's stubble might have worked better.

Being rejected as a juror is a piece of cake compared to being rejected romantically. I know. My friends have told me about it.

By being rejected romantically, we are talking about after the romance is underway and you are catapulted from it by your ex-love who gives you a reason which you believe he or she really means.

Rejections of this sort come in two flavors: Fixable and unfixable.

Fixable reasons are those qualities they don't like about you but that you could, if uncommonly moved to do so, fix. They include physical fitness, personal habits and addictions, ethics, the people you hang out with, your energy level, and how far away you live.

Unfixables are those you can't change no matter how much you want to. They include physical characteristics, personal history, race, ethnicity, handicaps, and religious upbringing.

There are laws that protect such people at the workplace and in public accommodations. But when it comes to romance, you're on your own.

People have a right to their own preferences. Normally, short Ethiopians don't get all misty-eyed over tall Eskimos, and wouldn't date them even if geography were not a problem. And that's okay. They get to chose. What's not okay is getting the other person hooked, then dropping on them the view that they are, after all, unqualified for reasons they can't change. Dirty pool.

Honesty within couples is admirable for the most part. But I have a problem when, in the name of truth, people who are close hurt each other in ways they would never hurt a stranger.

Unfixable rejections hurt most I think because there isn't a thing you can do about them. If you're five feet two, you can't, by dint of will and hard work, become six foot two. If your biological parents are Swedish, you can't become an ethnic Turk.

Nevertheless, in spite of rejection's pain, I think it's probably all for the best. Who cares what reason the rejectors give? If they say it's over, it's over — no matter whether it's fixable or not. There's no tie-breaker here. Whoever says "no way" first, wins. Besides, I can see a rejectee having an offending tattoo painfully and expensively removed, losing 50 pounds, and developing impressive muscle tone, only to be told, "and another thing I don't like about you..."

Priorities

A **friend once told me** her priorities in her marriage were (1.) her children, (2.) her husband, and (3.) herself.

She was there for all the soccer matches and the ballet recitals. She organized birthday parties, met with teachers, and hosted sleep-overs. She helped the children with their homework, mended their clothes, wiped their little noses, and tended to their every need. Only when she was certain they had been taken care of, did she turn her attention to her husband — ironed his shirts, cooked his favorite meals, took his car to be serviced, made his coffee, massaged his ego. Then when the children and her husband were taken care of, she took care of herself.

Or she would have, but there was no time left.

Now she's single again and has a job and a boyfriend. The priorities now are: (1.) the children, (2.) the job, (3.) a tie between the boyfriend and herself. And, big surprise, the boyfriend (third in a series) wants out. They spend an inordinate amount of their time together arguing. She thinks he doesn't understand motherhood and how important her kids are to her. And he thinks he's in the relationship all by himself.

54. - Single Over Thirty

When the woman described her priorities, I agreed with her. They seemed rather logical, even admirable and certainly ethical. In fact, the only flaw I could find is that they don't work. The things at the end of the list never get taken care of.

She probably needs to be more practical and less humble. Humble can hurt.

Take, for instance, standard procedures in the use of oxygen masks on airplanes. In case of an emergency, one is instructed to put one's own mask on first, then help your children. The logic is pretty obvious: If the child faints or becomes disoriented, you can put his mask on for him. But if you faint or become disoriented, you'd better have a guardian angel sitting in the next seat. It's certainly no time to be at the end of your own priority list. Your needs are greater than your children's. You are needed so you can help them and they don't need to help anybody.

I'm a great believer in need-driven priorities. That way, everyone gets to be number one. When my friend's children had a need, they should be number one and their needs taken care of. When her job has needs (from, say, 8:30 a.m. to 5 p.m. weekdays) they should be met. And when she has needs, by damn, she should be number one — a revolutionary idea for someone who has always put herself last. She deserves a life outside her work and her kids.

And my guess is that fulfilling those needs would take care of the boyfriend's needs too, unless, of course, he has some freakin' priority list of his own.

In the end, it shakes out much the same. Chances are my friend's kids will have the most needs. Her job will use up a predictable block of time. And she'll have fewer personal needs than the rest. The big difference is that those needs she does have will be taken care of. And, to use the oxygen mask analogy, she needs to survive to insure her kids do.

Taking appropriate care of one's own needs isn't selfish, it's utilitarian.

It promotes self esteem and a soaring spirit. And everyone benefits from that. Think about it. When you were a kid, would you rather have been raised by a fulfilled parent or a long-suffering martyr enslaved by her/his own guilt, humility and flawed priorities?

Speaking for myself, I would have rathered the former. But the latter might have been fun too — for a little while — just to see how much I could get away with.

Glue

G**yro's old girlfriend,** Nettie, once told him she loved him for his mind.

If thinking that made her happy, Gyro said, it was okay with him. But in the real world, she didn't know his mind. I doubt if he knew it himself. Perhaps she was just trying, as a lot of people do, to rise above that oft-maligned, mysterious, high-octane stuff called passion that had gripped them both and bonded them.

What is it that makes people apologize for the physical or, as it is often called, the mere physical? They liked each other, Gyro and Nettie, and they were a good fit. She had a fabulous sense of humor that delighted him. They both liked good music, and ballet, and foreign movies, and pate. But passion was the glue that held them together. I know a gazillion lovely, funny women who like pate. But they're unlikely matches for my friend Gyro.

If you've ever made a picture frame, you know what I mean. The pieces should be a good fit to begin with. And you'll need some glue, nothing rare or exotic, Elmer's will do. Then the two pieces, glue still sticky, should be clamped together and long brads hammered in to make the bond strong and, hopefully, permanent. Relationships are like that. Except that frames have four spars that need to be glued and relationships work best with just two people. Well, that was fairly safe. Who can deny that physical attraction plays a big part in couplings? Now for the hard part:

Question #1: How do you make it permanent, and

Question #2: How do you get it started when you and your intended are running low on glue, so to speak? And what about the brads that make the picture frame permanent? Shouldn't we extend the analogy to include the brads? If you've got long brads, why do you need glue?

Hah! I can see you've never really made a picture frame. I have tried it with brads and no glue and I'm here to tell you the picture frame is wobbly and eventually falls apart. So, do you still want to continue the analogy?

Do you want your relationship to be wobbly? I thought not. You need glue.

Now I'm going to attempt to answer the first two questions, but remember, I'm not an expert, just very opinionated.

Answer #1: You make it permanent by taking care of yourself, and by treating your partner with love, respect and understanding. And by being each other's friend and advocate.

Answer #2: The kind of glue we're talking about is manufactured in your head. If you run out, make some more. If you can't make some more, you probably are more interested in companionship that in coupling anyway.

And if that's the case, you might consider buying a dog. Or a goldfish.

Rituals

Orme and his live-in girlfriend, Sasha, are having a rocky time these days. But Orme's getting along famously with his dog.

He comes home from work and Fluffy is there to greet him, her tail wagging so hard it moves her whole back end. She sneezes with delight as he makes a fuss over her. "How's my little doggie? She's a good little doggie. Yes she is. Are you a good little doggie? Sure you are," he says bending down to scratch her back and bib. "Would my little doggie like a treat?"

He walks to the kitchen, opens the cupboard door and shakes a box of dog biscuits. Fluffy sneezes and wags and pants, on the edge of ecstasy.

He gives her a biscuit, then pets her back as she eats it happily.

"Where's your leash? Wanna go for a walk?" he says. Fluffy prances on the kitchen floor, her little paws clicking excitedly against the tiles.

Just then, Sasha walks in. Orme looks up. "Oh dear," he says, "I forgot to stop at the cleaners."

"Well, I'm going to need my turquoise blouse if we're going to the Thornton's tonight," she says.

He smiles good naturedly. "I'll go back and get it," he says. "Just as soon as I take Fluffy for a walk."

What's wrong with that picture?

Why does Orme seem to like his dog better than Sasha? Is it because Fluffy is a low-maintenance ally? Doesn't own a dry-clean-only blouse — or any blouse? Doesn't even wear clothes?

I don't think so.

I think it's because he and Fluffy have set up a ritual. And he and Sasha haven't. If they had, the scene might look like this:

Fluffy and Sasha hear the car door slam. They both arrive at the front door just as Orme opens it. While Fluffy wags, Sasha and Orme embrace.

"How was your day?" says Orme.

"Not bad at all," says Sasha. "Did you pick up my blouse from the dry cleaners?"

Orme snaps his fingers. "Damn. I forgot. I'll go back for it right after we have our coffee."

"I'm afraid they might close. How `bout if we go now? I'll go with you. We can have our coffee when we get back."

Watch the house, Fluffy," Orme says, "You're in charge."

The door closes leaving Fluffy alone, head cocked to one side, wondering when the door will open again. (She liked it better the other way.)

60. - Single Over Thirty

* * *

So how many Orme/Sasha rituals did you detect? If you found three, you got them all. They were:

1. Greeting each other at the door.

2. Having a ritual cup of coffee at the end of the work day.

3. Routinely running errands together (even thought it surely would be more efficient to run them singly.)

After the Fat Lady Sings

*Lives of Their Own * Still Friends * Time Went By * Single * Out-Smarted * Don't Call It Re-marriage * The Failure * Marrieds and Singles * The Long Run*

Lives of Their Own

My **friend Orme** wants to get married again. Actually, he decided that in 2001, but it just hasn't happened yet. Still he's hopeful, explaining that he's come close, but every time, he encounters some sort of weird obstacle he and the girl of his dreams can't surmount.

There was Anne, a successful lawyer who worked long hours and spent three days a week at her firm's Baltimore office. Orme is an accountant who is unavailable during tax season. They could never find enough time together. After increasingly longer periods of separation, they drifted apart.

Then there was Deb. She and Orme were going to move in together. Orme braced himself for her differing taste in art, wall hangings, furniture and knickknacks. But she wanted to supplant half the books in his book case. It had taken him most of his life to accumulate those books. He balked. She moved on.

Alice had two grown daughters and a son who consumed huge gobs of her time and attention. The daughters pretty much ignored Orme, and the son was openly hostile.

64. - Single Over Thirty

Then there was Paris who ran two miles before breakfast and told Orme if he didn't quit smoking she'd stop seeing him. He didn't and she did.

Orme never felt valued by Helena who had inherited a fortune from her parents, lived in a mansion the size of a subdivision, and threw money around like it was confetti.

Ruth seemed a good candidate. She was within a few years of Orem's age, intelligent, attractive, healthy, fit, successful, loving and well adjusted. And they hit it off. But the romance never went anywhere because, like the others, both she and Orme were subject to that cruel impediment to middle age get-togetherness: Lives of their own

Both had their own well established careers, skills, circle of friends, progeny, hobbies, memberships, expertise, habits, routines, possessions, judgments, experience (aka baggage), money and their very own ways of loading the dishwasher.

Had they met when they were in their early 20s, none of those would have been an issue. At that youthful age, they'd have been malleable. Their careers, hobbies, possessions and skills would have hardly begun to set. They'd have no complicating progeny; lots of opinions but few inflexible judgments, and most of their friends would be mutual classmates who were now scattered across the national landscape.

They would have had vacuous faces and vacuous lives; nothing much written on either one. Bending and adapting to form a couple would be a piece of cake.

My next door neighbor's son, aged five, is bi-lingual in Spanish and English. And though I've pretty much gotten the hang of English, I've been struggling with Spanish for years. Despite what you may be tempted to think, at age five my young neighbor is not my intellectual superior. The difference between us is that I already had a language in place when I started to learn Spanish. He had no such complicating mind-set.

Young romantics and my five-year-old neighbor have similar advantages. They both start with a relatively clean slate. The neighbor has no prior language that needs to be accommodated to learn Spanish; the romantics have no established lives in place that need to be re-ordered.

It's like building a new house in the attic of your existing one. It's possible, I suppose, but it's a lot easier to build it from the ground up.

Getting back to Orme: If he had met all those women when he and they were young and uncomplicated, would he have gotten together with Ruth, the best of the candidates? The answer is almost certainly "no" because one of the earlier ones would have surely snatched him up first.

Still Friends

When people say they are still friends with their old flames, what does that mean? Specifically, what do they mean by "friends?"

Do they call each other and discuss personal stuff like they do with other friends? Do they go places and do things together? Or does "friends" simply mean they don't bad-mouth each other. And when someone asks if they are still dating so-and-so, they reply, "No, but we're still friends."

How do they behave when they run into each other at social events — say a dance, or a discussion meeting? What if one of them has a date in tow?

I used to know the answers to those questions. It was simple. A friend was a friend. The fact that you no longer dated had little to do with it. If anything, the continued friendship was a validation of the old romance. It proved the romance was not a mere sexual attraction. There was a noble meeting of the minds and souls. Quality stuff. "See? Even after we've stopped dating, we remain devoted friends."

Then, I began to suspect my own motives. I noticed that I remained friends only with those to whom, on some level, I still was attracted. I did all the work and we remained friends. And for old flames in whom I had lost interest, I did no work and we lost touch.

There may be people who easily remain friends with old flames and are not bothered by seeing them cuddling with someone else. But that's outside my experience.

I concede that giving up old friends does not come easily. It's like trying to make yourself not care when, in fact, you do. Yet, continuing to work on the friendship after the romance has failed can be like showing up for a whippin'. At some point you ask, "What in the world am I doing this for? It hurts."

What I aspire to is a middle ground wherein one doesn't quit cold turkey. But when old flames begin to fade into the past, for goodness sake, let 'em.

Time Went By

Oh-oh, I think I'm becoming increasingly contented with my singlehood.

When I got divorced some years ago, I thought I'd quite naturally get married again, within a year, maybe two. I wondered what my new wife would be like. Would we have fun together; lose ourselves in long, insightful conversations? Would she sew buttons on for me? Would she be pleased when I brought her flowers? Would we figure our joint tax return and plan trips and vacations together? Would she get along with my kids? I dreamed-on about how fulfilling it could be in so many ways.

Then time went by.

At a singles discussion of "re-marriage", I said I might not marry again. I didn't mean it. I just said that to get a rise out of my friends at the meeting. And it worked. "Oh John, you'll marry again. That's for sure. Hey, don't worry about it. I'm surprised you haven't gotten married already..."

Then time went by.

At a high school reunion, I mentioned to one of my classmates I was divorced. "And you never re-married," she exclaimed in amazement.

"What do you mean *never*", I protested. "I just haven't yet."

Then time went by.

In another year at another singles discussion, I mentioned that I probably wouldn't get married again. No one commented. No one seemed surprised. And most telling, I wasn't surprised no one was surprised.

Then time went by and now I can hardly picture myself being married again. Imagine, I say to myself, going to bed at the same time someone else does.

Getting up in the morning and actually sitting down to breakfast with someone. Every day. Never again going to a singles function. No more dinners with women I've been fond of for years. Clearing it with someone else before accepting social invitations or spending money. Sharing the walls and bookshelves of my house with someone of differing tastes and history. Having feminine touches added to the decor of my hitherto masculine domain.

And then... and then I think again about how nice it would be to be loved and valued so much that someone wanted to share her life with me. Someone warm, soft and smooth and nice-smelling in my bed at night. Someone to exchange trivial thoughts and experiences with on a regular basis. Someone who has strengths and talents I lack and relishes those I have that she doesn't. Someone to hang a silk shorty nightgown in the closet.

And who knows, after we'd been coupled for a long time and had gotten increasingly closer, perhaps — just perhaps — I'd go to my closet one day, pull out a jacket, and find some sweet person had sewn on a new button.

Single

It was really quite simple when you were married, there were two kinds of people: Married and single.

Then you separated and, suddenly, you were neither. Or were you both? Your marriage license was still in effect, so you were married. But you were no longer half of a couple, so you were single. Then the divorce came through and you were truly, irrefutably, incontrovertibly single — free to mix it up with other singles.

Then the coupling process began all over. Or else it didn't. Perhaps you've had it with being part of a couple. Or perhaps you abhor going home alone and want to couple immediately. It is central to the newly single dilemma that you may want both at the same time.

Singledom/coupleness is a conundrum. What we need is someone who has not been corrupted by formal psychological and sociological training to sort all this out for us, someone like me. Here's my take on it:

Being single is an attitudinal sort of thing. You can see it play itself out in virtually any social function. That group of buzzing people hovering around the hors d'oeuvres can be divided into three types. Married. Single. And despairing.

If you think I exaggerate, get yourself invited to a party that includes someone's single friends and their married neighbors. You won't need a score card to tell which is which. Married people glom together like lactate clumps of curdled milk, automatically forming same-sex clusters to discuss the Redskins or comparison shopping.

The singles are the twinkley and witty ones who form coeducational clusters where the discussion topic is not as important as the cleverness of the banter. These people are clearly participants in THE HUNT — even if they're not aware of it.

Married people, on the other hand, know the hunt is over. They don't want to inadvertently begin a new hunt. They especially don't want to find an opposite sex person they are attracted to. Ergo, sports and home management topics prevail.

Despairing people of both genders are the recently uncoupled. They have been told by well-meaning friends that part of the cure for despair is to force one's wounded self into a social gathering. So they're there. In body at least.

Incidentally, joining the hunt doesn't necessarily mean a single wants to change his/her status. Sometimes, they just like hunting.

Despite my lack of formal training in such matters, I know about these things because I have, at one time or another, been married, single and despairing — as I suspect you have. Now at social functions, I join those twinkley, witty people who form coeducational clusters and don't give a damn about the Redskins — at least not until they start winning again.

Out-Smarted

When you think about it, ignorance isn't such a bad thing.

When I got married, I was 25 years old and not nearly as wise as I am today. The seeds of our future incompatibility were all over the place. But I didn't see them. And neither did my date/girlfriend/wife. So we fell in love and got married. Over the next two decades, we raised four of the nicest people you'd ever want to meet. And for much of that time, we were happy. Pretty dumb, huh?

If I'd been smart, like I am today, I'd have known better. We'd never have gotten together. I'd be looking for someone who met my needs better. ("*Needs*," by the way, hadn't been invented yet then, so you really can't blame me.) Certainly I'd have examined her Myers-Briggs scores for tell-tale signs of incompatibility. (M-B was also unknown then.) To make sure we really knew each other, we'd have discussed "*the relationship*" until we were nauseous. (They weren't called "*relationships*" then, of course. I don't know what they were called. Probably nothing.) We'd keep working at it until one of us found in the other the "fatal flaw." Then, of course, we'd have broken it off. After all, who wants to spend his/her life with someone who has a fatal flaw?

Anyone who is single over the age of thirty has probably heard a slew of horror stories about the half of the once-partnership that happens not to be present for the telling. We'd have to agree they're a pretty slimy lot.

But hearing is good. That's how we've gotten to be so smart — by listening to everyone's awful experiences. Now we can extrapolate potential faults and skullduggery we never would have imagined on our own.

The result is that we're now inordinately selective. We know what to look for. We're mature... and very experienced. We've had time to hone our people skills to a keen edge. We proudly proclaim our lofty standards and our uncompromising non-negotiables. Nobody's going to fool us. We know a thing or two about what makes people tick, what potential pitfalls to look for, and what mistakes to avoid. We are exceedingly wise in our judgements of the opposite sex. We're very discerning.

And very single.

Don't Call It Re-marriage

Call it a second marriage if you want, but don't expect it to be like the first. It's so different, it should have its own name.

Re-marriage sounds like you flunked it the first time so you're taking it over. I am not remarried, and therefore not an expert. Also I'm not a psychologist, psychiatrist, sociologist, counselor, or therapist. So, unencumbered by those inhibiting factors, I thought I'd take a shot at compiling a list those qualities that make re-marriage unique:

1. Unlike your first marriage, your new person already has a life. Expect a certain amount of allegiance to their existing employment, children, friends, avocations etc. The attachments may be so strong they'll be unbreakable. Try to pry them loose at your own peril.

2. The sex is better. Probably. Actually, it may not be, but it'll be different.

3. You'll never quite sort out all your second spouse's relatives the way you did your first's. Because of the passage of time, you're less likely, for instance, to get to know the grandparents-in-law and perhaps even the parents-in-law. Or to care that much about the others. You may wonder why you committed so many relatives to memory the first time around. Come to think of it, why did you?

4. Reminders of the first marriage will be everywhere. Favorite melodies, deja vu experiences, children, knick-knacks that had their genesis in the first marriage, alimony checks. The list goes on and they'll be scattered about like coffee grounds in the sink of life, as one of my re-married friends likes to put it.

5. Expect pockets of hostility in the most unexpected places. — Like having you and your spouse seated on the periphery of a family wedding dinner while your ex (no relation to the bride or groom) sits with your siblings.

6. You know too much to expect perfection and that colors the relationship. One of the things you know this time is that you're not looking for a mate with no faults, you're looking for a mate with faults you can live with.

7. Some people, perhaps even your children, will actually be happy for you and rejoice in your obvious new-found happiness.

8. Some people will be happy for you because they abhor the single state like nature abhors a vacuum. They would rejoice even if you married a tea set.

9. Because there are usually no children forthcoming in the second marriage, there is less need for the state to protect the children's interests. The law, therefore, doesn't need to be as involved. Nor does religion. Nor the neighborhood. Nor your in-laws. They all will be, of course, but it's not as necessary as it was the first time and therefore may seem less intrusive.

10. You'll live in neutral territory, a house for both of you. Not your place and not his/hers. Don't be surprised if half your books, half your linens, half your wall hangings, and half your furniture are supplanted.

11. There'll be fewer bumpy spots, less uncharted territory, not as many seemingly unsolvable problems as the first time because you're now more experienced, richer and smarter.

12. There'll be new problems you never experienced in your first marriage and never could have predicted and no amount of experience, wealth or wisdom will prepare you for them.

13. You're more likely to marry someone of divergent ethnicity, age, religion, race, educational level, and political views.

14. Now that you are older and more experienced, you are likely to bring more baggage to the second union. On the plus side, you have had more time to process it.

15. The new marriage will be a new experience, not a reliving of the old. Different person. Different times. Different stage of your life. Different age. Different priorities. Different responsibilities. Different friends, perhaps. My in-expert advice is to treat the new marriage as something entirely new, remembering the adage:

"If you always do what you always did,

You'll always get what you always got."

The Failure

I know I promised my newly separated friend I wasn't going to be a know-it-all, but that was before he said he felt he was a failure.

In my view, it can be a formidable task for people to live their whole adult lives based on a decision made as kids (early 20s) when they were brimming with inexperience, rampant optimism, and testosterone.

And that's not exactly an original view. In a television interview several years ago, Clare Boothe Luce told Dick Cavett that ideally everybody ought to get married three times in their lifetimes, once for youthful passion, once for raising a family, and once for companionship. The thought that one person will fit all three roles in turn is a bit of a stretch, she said.

That scenario seems a bit extreme to me - and maybe it did to Ms. Luce too. For 32 years, she was married to Henry Luce, founder of Time magazine. Maybe she was just trying to be an interesting guest on the Dick Cavett Show. But there is some undeniable logic in what she said. (Clare Boothe Luce was variously a globe-trotting journalist, a Congresswoman from Connecticut, ambassador to Italy and briefly Brazil, and a leading American playwright

78. - Single Over Thirty

In a moment of pique she once quipped publicly that Sen. Wayne Morse's actions were the result of his being "kicked in the head by a horse." That observation, incidentally, explains why she was only briefly ambassador to Brazil.)

But getting back to my friend, "the failure," he was president of his high school senior class, attended an Ivy League college, had a successful career in publishing, and with his wife, raised three loving daughters all of whom went on to get their PhDs. And through it all he was (and is) a gentle, thoughtful soul.

Regardless of how he may feel, that's not the track record of a screw-up.

All this points up the dangers of making promises - especially those life-shaping ones you want to keep and are sure you will. There are times when the only sensible thing to do is to go back on your word. Ouch! Did they really think in their early 20s that they would remain a couple forever? Yes, they did. Probably. Certainly, I thought I would.

In my aforementioned role as a know-it-all, I'll tell you how this entanglement gets started. When one is in one's late teens or early 20s, Providence chooses one person out of the billions who inhabit the earth and plunks them down in, for instance, the seat next to one in one's English Literature class. For people in their late teens or early 20s, a sort of benign insanity then moves in like an early morning fog. And that's a good thing. Think about it. Somebody has to completely repopulate the earth every 80 years or so. Trust me, it's an important job. And it's plainly not gong to get done if these virile young people ignore each other.

So young and inexperienced as they may be, they commit to a life together. What's more, they actually tell people about it. They make believers of themselves, their sweethearts, their parents, their clergy, a church full of well wishers, the IRS, the mortgage company, the world. And sometimes that commitment holds. But half the time, it doesn't.

The census bureau says 82 million men and women in the United States are unmarried, including 20 million divorced adults, 13.6 million who are widowed, and 48 million who have never married -- not yet anyway. Half of all U.S. households are headed by unmarrieds; 36 percent of the work force, and 36 percent of those who voted are unmarried.

More than half of those Americans between 15 and 85 will spend more years single than married, it is projected.

So my newly separated friend is not alone. And he's a long way from being a failure. Reentering singledom after all these years is not entirely his doing. Nature stacked the deck.

Married and *Singles*

Married people, women particularly, tend to begin their letters with "Dear John," and end them with "Love, Elizabeth." By contrast, single people, so as not to be misunderstood, begin with "Hi John" and end with something like "Later, Elizabeth."

There must be other characteristics that distinguish married people (70 percent of the U.S. population over 35) from single people (30 percent).

A growing number of books and treatises examine the differences in style between men and women, but I haven't been able to find any such comparison between marrieds and singles. So, naturally, I made one up. There's an openness about single people that I like. And a smugness about some married people that annoys me. Or do I just imagine that because I'm single?

Studies have shown that marrieds are psychologically better off, richer, happier, less pone to suicide, more successful in their careers, healthier, and that they live longer. I know that's true because my married friends have told me so. They probably also have bigger houses, faster cars and whiter teeth.

I worried about those findings for a time, then it dawned on me: Of course. Everybody wants to marry someone with longevity who's sane, rich, cheerful, successful, healthy and unlikely to precipitously "off" himself/herself. But such people probably developed those characteristics as singles — then got married. Chalk one up for our side. Next time, *we'll* conduct the study.

Here's a better way to determine marital status: Let's say you go to a restaurant and see two couples. One is chatty and animated; the other eats in silence barely looking at each other. Which would you guess is the married couple? Perhaps it's the difference between a dinner date (for singles) and simply the cook's night off (for marrieds).

At parties, I notice married men are likely to congregate in all-male clusters and talk typically about sports, lawn care and computers. Women, about children, shopping, and their husbands. Singles gather in co-ed groups and laugh a lot. They discuss feelings, ideas, and events. Perhaps marrieds don't want to give their partners reason, real or imagined, to be jealous.

The studies claim singles have more sex than marrieds. Yeah, right. Even if sex isn't as much fun for marrieds, it's so convenient that unattached singles would have a hard time keeping up the pace. And how do they conduct those studies anyway? No one asked me. If they had, I'd have lied.

Harvard anthropologist Peter Gray conducted a recent survey of the saliva of 58 men and found that married men produced less testosterone than unmarried men and both had more of the male sex hormone than married men with children. The study theorizes that lowering of married men's testosterone may be nature's way of keeping them faithful and at home.

82. - Single Over Thirty

I suppose once a man says "I do", his testosterone level drops precipitously, much like the re-sale value of a new car once you drive it off the lot.

The Harvard survey goes on to speculate testosterone levels may be affected by parenting the same way tests have shown that winning or losing in sports affects hormone levels.

There's no mention in the study of single parents. Then again, the study may prove that one's testosterone stops rising to the level of one's saliva when one is married and concentrates, instead, in more appropriate places. Another study shows that married women are more likely than single women to be heavy users of facial cosmetics, and the difference by marital status is mostly among middle-aged women. I thought you'd want to know.

Single people are much more likely to be the subject of TV sitcoms. And the more dysfunctional, the better. Married people, I have noticed, change after marriage. They learn to role-play and they get very good at it, seldom stepping out of character.

The guy I bought my house from was showing me how to refill the hot tub when his wife chimed in with "We refill the tub with fresh water every month."

"Nah," the husband disdained, "We refill it once every six months."

"That's right," says the wife, "We refill it every six months."

I hate that. He plays an arrogant bully who is never wrong and she plays the submissive wimp who swears to what her husband says no matter what.

If he were single, no one but a masochist would put up with his insolent, disrespectful demeanor. He almost certainly wasn't like that when he wooed and won his wife.

You may have noticed this column is fraught with generalizations. I admit it. Certainly some singles are so flawed, it must be obvious to the whole world that they are not single out of choice. And, conversely, with some marrieds, there's a joy and togetherness that's enviable. Having someone who is one's full-time advocate must be nice. If it's done right and doesn't get to be the bully and the submissive, it can be very rewarding.

Given enough time together, two married people can almost merge into one as demonstrated in that famous New Yorker cartoon depicting a middle aged couple studying the menu at a restaurant. The woman is asking, "Which one of us is it that doesn't like asparagus?"

The Long Run

Everybody knows that couples are supposed to get along together for a long, long time. And some actually do. They don't fight, or ignore each other or split. I think I have found one such couple, in it for the long run and loving it.

They're in their seventies, the obelisk and the globe. He's tall and willowy with a thatch of tangled white hair sitting above his lined face like an albino rabbit. She's short and round and cheerful with little sprays of white poking out from her otherwise dark hair. They're a couple. They've been a couple for half a century, ever since he was 23 and she was 20.

She is still on her guard lest any other women deign to show an interest in him. What is she thinking about? He's long and skinny and old and stiff. He falls asleep in his chair, particularly in the evenings. She need not worry. It's safe to take him to the mall on a Saturday afternoon. The teenie boppers will leave him alone. Promise.

There they are in the evening sitting around their living room talking with friends. He's at one end of the sofa, she's at the other. She kicks off her shoes and puts her stockinged feet on the sofa between them. He picks up one foot and begins to gently massage it. The conversation never misses a beat. No one is surprised. That's the way they are.

He makes a bold, opinion statement. She disagrees and states the opposite view. No retort comes back. He doesn't take her opposing position personally. Her tone was not confrontational. He does not feel attacked. Neither is defensive. Two people stated two differing opinions. So what's wrong with that? Neither expects to be agreed with all the time.

She doesn't pout. He doesn't bully. She doesn't nag. He doesn't posture. Neither criticizes, rebukes, belittles or otherwise diminishes the other. They're equal partners and they seem to actually like each other. They laugh a lot.

She made two trips to Europe with her church group. He didn't want to go, but there was no question that she would go anyway. She is very social, belongs to a bridge club, regularly has lunch with her women friends, helped organize her high school reunion, and seldom misses church on Sunday mornings. He sleeps-in on Sundays, spends hours doing carpentry and crafts in his basement workshop, and happily accompanies her to high school reunions without actually contributing to their organization.

If I showed the foregoing to them, they'd be embarrassed. They'd say I was idealizing their marriage -- that there were a lot of bumps along the way that I don't know about. And of course they'd be right. I don't know about their bumps. I don't even want to.

What have they been doing all these years that has kept them so comfortable with each other? I doubt that they have a formula. They don't seem like the type to set up rules of behavior, then follow them. So I have to conclude that there are two key elements:

The first is that each has a generous attitude. That means their first response is to give, to allow, to contribute, to accommodate, to share, to protect.

The second element is luck. Each is lucky that the other has a generous attitude too.

*Concepts * Speed Dating * The Early Demise of Real Men * Singles Weekends * Intriguing Differences * Myers-Briggs * The Rules*

Concepts

I **had a discussion** the other day with an expert. He has a Ph.D. in behavioral psychology. We were discussing the mind.

I told him that some years ago I wrote a program for stopping smoking without having to use excessive will power. In nutshell, the premise of the program was that the desire to stop smoking is lodged in the conscious mind and the habit is in the subconscious mind. And the two minds respond to different sets of instructions. So to root out the habit, one must address the subconscious mind.

As an expert in the field, he assured me that humans only have one mind and the success of my program was probably attributable to the fact that people already wanted to stop — long before reading my "inexpertise." I said that since the mind isn't real, one can have as many minds as one damned well pleases. And it pleases me to have two.

Whereas the brain is real, the mind is a concept. It has no weight, shape, color, volume or position in time. It's an abstraction we humans concocted to explain how we use our brains to react, survive, discriminate, create ideas, access memory, and figure our taxes.

90. - Single Over Thirty

Here is a sample list of things that are real and those that are not:

— Money is real. Wealth is a concept.
— Events are real. Memories of them are concepts.
— Sound is real. Music is a concept.
— Voices are real. Language is a concept.
— Men and women are real. Love is a concept.
— Food is real. Taste is a concept.
— Empty rooms are real. Loneliness is a concept.
— Behavior is real. Rules are concepts.
— History is real. Written accounts of it are concepts.
— Snow is real. Winter weather is a concept.
— You are real. Your name is a concept.

Virtually all discussions are about concepts. It's no fun and only marginally rewarding to discuss real things. The fun is in the concepts.

The fact that concepts are not real should not diminish their importance. Refining the concepts is, in large measure, what life's experience is about. And dismissing them as "mere concepts" can be folly.

I don't want to take this thing too far. Surely someone can catch me up on some ambiguity. My point is, however, that experts have a way of closing down the thought process and inhibiting free and open discussion. It wasn't my Ph.D. friend's dismissal of my two-minds concept that put me off. I sort of expected that. After all, he had turf to defend. It was the reaction of the third party in that discussion who, after hearing the expert's pronouncement, utterly invalidated both of my minds, my program, its effectiveness, my right to devise it, the people who had taken it, me, and the horse I rode in on.

I think I like it better when an expert just listens, raises a quizzical eyebrow and says something like, "Well, that's one theory."

Speed Dating

Why didn't I think of that? Speed dating. Equal numbers of men and women meet in a room. You talk to each person of the opposite sex for six minutes. Or you stare at each other stupidly. Or make faces. It doesn't matter. After six minutes, you're on to the next person for six minutes.

When it's all over, you decide who you'd like to get to know better and you turn their names in to the proctor who is sworn to secrecy. If you want to see a person who also wants to see you, the proctor will send each of you the other's phone number. If you want to see the other and the other doesn't want to see you, the other never gets to know you expressed an interest.

Whereas, technically, one may get rejected from time to time, it's painless. The rejecter never learns that the rejectee was interested.

That's how it works in theory — safely, quietly, anonymously, and without the possibility of embarrassment. What a great idea. What a terrific topic for a Single-Over-Thirty column.

So I signed up on the Internet and paid $25 by credit card,

(proceeds went to the Red Cross) then showed up on a Saturday afternoon at the huge outdoor atrium smack in the middle of a bustling shopping mall. A gazillion curious shoppers marched by pushing their strollers, swinging shopping bags and gawking at the strange arrangement of people and tables in the middle of the mall.

So much for anonymity. Utopia begins to crumble. Men and women participants milled around at the entrance to the atrium, obviously embarrassed. All they needed were signs that said "single and desperate." They tried not to make eye contact with each other or anybody else.

Thirty tables, each with two chairs, were spread about the atrium floor in three groups of ten, arranged by the age of participants. A woman sat at each table with an empty chair. Then the men were let loose and sat at the table designated on their first-name-only name tags. In theory, they had six minutes to visit. In fact, they had less time because some of the 60-minute total was used up making sure everyone understood the rules and was properly seated.

Then it began. And it was fine. The ten women I talked with were all charming, nice people. (The men seemed less spiffy, some dressed in shorts, sandals and baseball caps.) Then, in six minutes, it was time to move on to the next table. Five minutes later we moved again. The next seemed to take about three (they were making up time) and the others fell far short of six.

You were supposed to jot down only the names of those who interested you as you sat at the table with them. And still keep it a secret? Am I missing something here? Wouldn't the other person notice? I wrote down everyone's name so as not to blatantly reject anyone in their presence, then after I had made the full tour, I crossed out those I wasn't interested in.

I hadn't intended to write anyone's name down except the woman friend I had come with, but one woman interested me, so I wrote her name too.

Chaos ensued. It was unclear how to write the names, who to give the cards to, or how to receive the results. Were we supposed to wait for the results?

We waited, searched and eventually found the person who had our cards. When she handed me mine, she said in a rather public voice, "Sorry, you didn't have any matches."

So much for secrecy.

My friend Orme used to boast that he always tried to figure whether a woman was interested before he asked her out. If he thought she'd say no, he wouldn't ask, thereby avoiding rejection.

Speed dating seemed a bit like that. A safe, innovative way to avoid rejection. It should have felt terrific. So why didn't it? It was awkward, even embarrassing, standing there with a bunch of strangers who you were only supposed to talk with for six minutes at a designated table at a designated time. You weren't to ask their last names. And then there were all those mall people walking around. You'd think it was their mall. Actually, it was. What must they be thinking? What ever happened to privacy?

I still wonder about the woman who wasn't interested when I was. As she left (before I knew she hadn't put my name down) she looked back and waved. I was so sure. Maybe she got the names confused. Maybe the tabulators mis-tabulated. Maybe if we'd had the full six minutes... Maybe if we'd met at a dance...

So much for avoiding feelings of rejection.

The Early Demise of Real Men

Women live six years longer than men do. The early demise of men is what the American Heart Assn. calls "an uncontrollable risk factor."

They're wrong.

Men die early because they do it to themselves.

There was a time in the early 1900s when men and women lived to the same average age: 48 years. Children and young adults died of diseases like diphtheria, tuberculosis, dysentery, pneumonia and flu. Those men and women who reached 50 could expect, on average, another 20 years or so. Now men live to an average of 74, women to 80. Think about it. Since the turn of the 20th century, women have managed to live six years longer than men.

How do they do that?

They don't. Women don't really live six years longer; men just die six years earlier. There's a difference. And it has to do with the "real man" attitude.

Compared to women (who are no angels themselves), real

men statistically:

-- Are less likely to eat a healthy diet.
-- Don't take vitamin supplements.
-- Don't get regular physical exams. (Hey, Rambo doesn't submit to proctology for anybody.)
-- Get less exercise.
-- Are more fatalistic. ("When your time comes, there isn't anything you can do about it.")
— Suffer more from depression. (Middle aged men commit suicide at a rate five times that of middle-aged women.)
— Don't have a clue what their blood pressure or cholesterol levels are.
— Ignore chronic aches and pains, opting to tough it out instead of seeking medical help.
— Are more likely to be the victims of war, disease and violence.

Compared to women, real men drink too much, drive too fast, shun vitamins and sunscreen, eat too much fat, and don't eat enough fiber. And any one of those can be fatal.

There was a time not too long ago when it was politically incorrect to admit there were significant attitudinal and behavioral differences between men and women. That mental set prevented otherwise enlightened people from looking at the effect of those differences.

Sun bathing is a good example.

Prof. Will Courtney of Sonoma State University in California, reports that men are twice as likely as women to die from melanoma, the most serious form of skin cancer, because they don't take the same precautions women do.

Though more women than men sunbathe (27 percent vs.

23 percent), Courtney reports, men spend more time in the sun and use sunscreen and protective clothing a quarter as often. Although self examination may prevent melanoma infections, only 43 percent of men discover their own lesions, compared with 62 percent of women. There is, remarkably, one new medical advance that is prompting more men to see their doctors and discuss hitherto "private" concerns: Viagra. An astute physician can often connect a patient's impotence to underlying causes such as untreated diabetes, hypertension, alcohol abuse or chronic depression — potentially life-threatening conditions for which the men would otherwise not have sought medical help.

Women, of course, are no idols of perfect health practices either. Most maintain harmful life styles too; it's just a matter of degree. In fact, there is one statistic in which women come out with the worst record. Beyond the age of 75, more women than men experience heart attacks.

Most men, of course, are already dead by then.

Singles Weekends

In passing, I mentioned to my long-married friend, Edmund, that I was going away on a singles week-end.

"Ooooh, wow," he panted, "That's faaantastic. Going to the mountains to party with a bunch of single people. Whoopee-ding. You lucky dog."

"No no no," I said. "It's not what you think. It's just a week-end with friends. And it'll be fun. But not 'whoopee-ding' fun. No hankey-pankey.".

"Come on," he said. "Everyone knows you single people have affairs all the time."

"Single people don't have affairs," I said. "They have rela-tionships. Married people have affairs. You can't have an affair if you don't have a spouse. It's a rule."

"Right," he said. "All you single people sharing the same coed houses away in a mountain resort. Guzzling wine. Massage parlors. Naked hot tub parties. Wild dancing to the beat of jungle music. No children around to cramp your style. And I suppose you want me to believe you sit around playing Scrabble and singing hymns".

98. - Single Over Thirty

"No hymns," I said.

Should I tell him what singles weekends are really like? Would he believe me if I did? Do I care?

In truth, the weekend was more like the movie, 'The Big Chill,' than the bawdy affair he envisioned -- without the dead body, of course.

Those of us who attended were mostly friends whose personalities, ethics and behaviors didn't undergo a ribald change for the weekend. Nobody got publicly drunk, naked, or predacious.

The first evening, about 60 revelers converged upon the host cabin to visit, chat, laugh, sample hors d'oeuvres, drink wine, beer and soft drinks, and dance in front of the massive stone fireplace to the musical beat of a boom box. As the evening progressed, visitors slowly drifted back to their own cabins until, by midnight, only the people from the host cabin remained -- and half of them had already gone to bed. A few sat around afterwards with a final glass of wine, discussing the behavioral differences between men and women.

"What a snooze," my married friend Edmund would surely have said - if I told him the truth - which I was not planning to do.

One volunteer in each cabin made breakfast the next morning, after which the avid hikers among us charged up the mountain followed by a smaller group of less-avid hikers who, equipped with a little green reference book, examined wild flowers along the way at a more leisurely pace.

After a pick-up lunch from each cabin's well-provisioned refrigerator, some people headed for the hot tubs (with suits), swimming pools, work-out rooms, or the massage parlor, while others walked the grounds, biked, cabin hopped, or sat around chatting, playing board games, or napping. Others went antiquing, or played golf, tennis, or volley ball. Or they went horseback riding or canoeing or bird watching.

A small contingent of revelers, of course, had to hurry back to the cabin to prepare for the shared dinner. By prior arrangement, each cabin had been matched with another cabin; one as host and one as guest. Each cabin prepared half the meal which they all shared at the host cabin.

After dinner, it was another party. This time the center piece was a sing-along in one of the cabins. But the sing along had competition. Someone played salsa music on the boom box and a group danced to it endlessly. And Rose brought a couple of tapes of "Sex and the City," which attracted a crowd of two dozen women sardined into her bedroom. Michael, daring soul that he is, walked into the room during mid show and reclined on Rose's bed surrounded by giggling women. It took his girlfriend, Nancy, less than three minutes to find him and drag him out of there.

The next day it rained, so the second, more vigorous hike was cancelled. We visited a local winery instead. In the evening, each cabin contributed to a dessert party.

The final morning, we made breakfast from leftovers. Everyone handed in their receipts for food and supplies bought for the weekend and we settled up. All the left-over food was put on the dining room table. People took what they wanted and we threw out the rest, then went home.

The next time I saw my married friend Edmund, he had a gleam in his eye. "So how'd the singles weekend go?" he whispered conspiratorially.

"Same ol' same ol'," I said. "Naked dancing, bed hopping, drunken reveling."

"Hah!" he said. "Just as I thought."

Intriguing Differences

Here's my premise: In everyday life, you get along best with people who are like you. But you are most likely to fall in love with someone who is different.

If my premise is true, you may ask, why do Internet dating services -- like E-mode and Match Dot Com -- put so much emphasis on finding your "perfect match?"

I think it's because it's easier for them to measure similarities and nearly impossible to measure intriguing differences.

Typically, dating services ask a gazillion questions about your habits, preferences, passions, reading materials, movie favorites, recreational activities, age, body type, ethnicity, history, style, talents, creativity, sexual personality, tastes, values, fears, IQ, subconscious thoughts, and about 30 other characteristics. All these questions are fed into a computer which spits out answers directed at finding your perfect match.

Why find your match? You're unlikely to be smitten by them anyway. And who's to say the dating services know what they're doing or that their tests and quizzes are valid?

Luckily for you, almost no one is your perfect match. And anyone who is nearly a match, will probably bore you to tears.

According to the experts, real people are romantically attracted to each other on the basis of their differences, not their similarities. And that sounds a responsive chord with me. The last person I would want to couple with is someone who is just like me. If I'm shy, I'd like someone who is extroverted. If I tend to be intense, I'd get along best with someone who is relaxed. I'd like my strengths to be mine and hers to be hers. I don't want us to be in competition to see who can remember the most Shakespeare from high school. Or who can most easily unscrew the lid from a pickle jar.

Although we might both like music and, in fact, like to perform, I'd just as soon she played the piano to my violin or sang to my accompaniment. Okay, in some cases, a duet might work - better if one sang melody and the other, harmony.

When I was in college, I was mesmerized by a lovely coed who was on the women's water ballet team -- and it wasn't all because she looked so fetching in a bathing suit. I marveled over her ability to swim with such ease, grace and proficiency. To a splasher like me, it seemed like pure, syncopated magic. I also liked that she was blonde to my dark hair -- and that she had blue eyes, not brown like mine. And unlike me, she was a good student and could knit a sweater, sing on key, and whip up pancakes without looking at a cook book.

We were good friends and alike in many ways. And I appreciated the similarities. But it was the differences that intrigued me and sparked my passion. (To my great disappointment, right after graduation she married a Lutheran minister from her home town.)

102. - Single Over Thirty

There is an excitement about someone whose interests and talents are different than one's own. But the benefits of not being a perfect match don't end there. The best couplings complement each other by filling one's weaknesses with the other's strengths. It also levels the playing field, making the partners equal -- each with his/her own special abilities . It discourages the "alpha dog" syndrome in which one half of the couple is always right and always prevails.

Still, one should choose one's differences carefully. If one needs to live in the country and the other the city, that's not good. If one is a born-again Christian and the other a devout Jew, finding a middle ground may be a chore. If one can't live without his/her cats and the other is allergic to them, they've got a problem. If one practices baseball after work weekdays and plays competitively on weekends, togetherness can be a pipe dream.

But keeping that kind of exception in mind, look for the differences. They don't have to be earth-shaking differences. Just differences. And, since you won't find them on the Internet dating services, here's a list you can pick and choose from. Assuming these are not already your strong suit, you may be intrigued by someone who...

1. Can read street signs from several blocks away.

2. Is tall enough to reach the top shelf.

3. Keeps track of household finances.

4. Actually likes to shovel snow.

5. Has a green thumb.

6. Is a computer whiz.

7. Is a born story teller.

8. Is double jointed.
9. Can perform magic tricks.
10. Can easily start a fire in the fireplace and keep it going.
11. Is a neatnik.
12. Can fly an airplane.
13. Does a great Arnold Schwarzenegger imitation.
14. Makes a perfect martini.
15. Plays the guitar.
16. Can resist chocolate candy.
17. Fixes small appliances.
18. Sees the big picture.
19. Is artistic.
20. Has a good sense of direction.
21. Is a good speller.
22. Grooves on your differences.

Myers-Briggs

It all started when Katherine Myers noticed her daughter's new husband, attorney Clarence Briggs, was different than the rest of the family.

So she and her daughter, neither of whom was trained in psychology, became fascinated with personality types. Katherine, the mother, introduced her daughter, Isabel, to Carl Jung's book, Psychological Types. And soon mother and daughter became avid "type watchers." They took their new avocation very seriously, seeing in it an opportunity to help ordinary people understand themselves and each other better. To that end, they devised a simple (though long) multiple choice test based on one's preferences. They asked questions like "At parties, do you (a) stay late, with increasing energy or (b) leave early, with decreased energy?" And "Are you more impressed by (a) principles or (b) emotions."

Pretty easy test and there are no wrong answers. It's all about preferences. Nobody tries to read your subconscious, alter your behavior, or pass judgment. Staying at a party late with increased energy, for instance, may be a sign of an extrovert. But it doesn't by itself make one an extrovert. In fact, Jung said no one is a total extrovert. (Of course, he didn't know my Uncle Jake after he's had two beers.)

There's nothing quite like the Myers-Briggs test. It's been around now for more than 40 years and the test is still taken by a whopping two million people a year. Countless employers routinely give the test to new employees in an effort to more effectively use the employee's special talents and interests -- and to better avoid personality conflicts

I first took the test enroute to a singles weekend several years ago. My passenger, a sweet woman named Robyn, read the questions to me as I drove. When we arrived at our destination, we discovered we were just about opposites. In Myers-Briggs parlance, she was an introvert to my extrovert; sensing to my intuitiveness; a thinker to my feeler, and judging to my perceiving.

No wonder we found each other so fascinating. It was like having one's own personal extra terrestrial to pal around with.

There are people who won't date anyone with certain Myers-Briggs scores because they fear it would be a bad match. While others, like me, think the Myers-Briggs test is simply a means to understanding the other - and one's self. Robyn was such a nice person, I wasn't at all put off by our differences - which were considerable. She once spent an hour finding a seven-cent imbalance in her check book. If I'd had the same problem, I'd have said, "close enough," and moved on. Differences like that seem rather harmless to me. Of course, we could have created a problem if she'd insisted I balance my checkbook every day or if I'd insisted she let hers slide.

In 1978, David Keirsey and Marilyn Bates published a fabulous book called “Please Understand Me” that put the Myers-Briggs test in virtually anyone's hands. It includes an abbreviated version of the test and a detailed description of the characteristics of each of the 16 personality types.

106. - Single Over Thirty

When I read my description, I thought "How'd they know that?" Of course, they knew it because I told them by answering that seemingly endless list. The descriptions were quite detailed and precise - nothing like horoscopes, for instance, where even those descriptions that weren't under my astrological sign sometimes seem to fit me just fine.

The principal message of "Please Understand Me", is hard to miss:

Abandon those endless, fruitless attempts to make people conform. Don't try to change people -- not your significant other, not your children, not your co-workers.

Or, put another way, don't think you can make a lion into a house cat by removing its teeth. All you'll get is a toothless lion with an attitude.

The Rules

Not since the impromptu tour of the girls' (unoccupied) locker room at our high school reunion last summer have I felt so much like I was invading women's private domain.

Yes, I read "The Rules," a best seller in which two women tell all single women how to intrigue men into marriage. The authors' credentials: They're married and you're not.

The book is not intended to be funny. The authors project and earnest, evangelical zeal aimed at returning women to the good old ways. But it's so outrageous, it's difficult to keep a straight face. It's like a serious book on fashion that counsels people to put their socks on over their shoes.

Don't look at men. Act disinterested. Never call a man and seldom return his calls. And, my personal favorite: Don't discuss The Rules with your therapist because he/she may think the rules are dishonest and manipulative.

Even people who say they like the book are quick to add which rules they don't follow. Those naive enough to follow all the rules all the time may never have another date, let alone get married. But that's okay. People like that probably shouldn't multiply anyway.

108. - Single Over Thirty

The Rules is a book for the clueless written by the really clueless. The idea seems to be to return to pre-feminist mind games, exploiting the male hunting urge by playing hard to get.

Unlike Debra Tannen, author of "Please Understand Me," from original research, and John Gray, who wrote "Men Are From Mars...," from other people's research, these authors wrote from a sort of "spontaneous knowing." They just wrote down what had been, until a half-century ago, a common behavioral practice among straight-lacedwomen.

So much for my unbiased, open-minded and objective review of the book. Now for my personal views:

Most of the rules would make me head for the hills. If a woman acts as if she doesn't want to go out, I don't ask her again. If she always hangs up first, and doesn't return calls, I stop calling. If she shows no initiative, ends evenings prematurely, and is always busy, I take that as a message to look elsewhere. And I do.

Are you surprised?

The book's contention that early-on use of the rules would prevent abusive behavior by a husband is a bit of a stretch. Abuse is levied by abusive people. And nice people — whether or not they've been subjected to "The Rules" retrogression — don't abuse anyone.

It's only fair to point out that, after the first 73 infuriating pages of bad advice, the authors begin to give good advice. They recommend practicing safe sex, maintaining high self-esteem, not rushing into intimacy, being social and involved, etc. My theory is that they had about 73 pages of archaic rules dredged up from the unenlightened past. But it's difficult to get publishers to print a 73-page book, so they winged it for the next 103 pages with tried-and-true common-sense advice everyone else has been plugging for decades.

*What Do Men Think? * Women Talk * Fear * Eye Contact * Burdenless * Shopping * Too Fussy * Choice * Fantasy * Libido * Life Is a Dance Floor * Crying * Cup of Tea * Hero * Men and Women*

What Do Men Think?

Picture this: You have an opposite-sex pal. A buddy. No romance going on there, thanks, just good ol' friends who can talk about anything. Having a friend like that is pure magic; privileged access to the other gender's psyche. Oh the power of it all.

Sophie was my opposite-sex friend. Still is, but it's just not the same anymore. She gave me a woman's point of view and, when I gave my opinion, she seemed to hang on to my every word. Then one day it changed forever. As we were discussing a particularly critical topic, she asked, "What do men think?"

And I said I didn't know.

"But you're a man," she said observantly.

Perhaps you can imagine how tempted I was to say, "Oh yeah, I forgot." and presume to speak for all men. But I didn't. I'm only one man. And we men are all different. I only know what I think — and even that keeps changing. We're a gender, not a club.

A club, now there's a thought. It's probably too late for Sophie and me, but maybe a club's not such a bad idea.

112. - Single Over Thirty

We men could all get together and savvy this thing out. Sort of a World Congress of Men. We could set up a charter that describes, definitively, exactly what we men think.

It'd be fun. We'd meet in a very male place like a pool hall or a biker bar and pass a series of resolutions; a charter of male preferences and beliefs. I can see it now: "All in favor of leaving the toilet seat up, signify by saying aye. All those opposed to asking for directions, raise your right hand. Those in favor of looking women in the eye when talking to them..."

Here, based on sociological research into common male behavior, is a sampling of some of the resolutions we might pass to prevent men like me from disappointing women like Sophie:

Resolution #1. — *Beer vs. wine.* Beer drinking is preferred unless (1.) you run out, (2.) the host has put out wine and hidden the beer in the back of a neighbor's refrigerator, and (3.) there is an "Out of Order" sign on the only available bathroom. The World Congress favors beer for those who drink and is considering a series of pro-beer public service TV spots fashioned after the popular orange juice commercials. The slogan will be "Beer — It's not just for breakfast any more."

Resolution #2. — *Asking for directions.* Men are not required to stop and ask for directions no matter how lost they are, how late it gets, or how frustrated their dates become. Asking for directions is deemed to be unmasculine and a clear sign of wobble. Can you imagine John Wayne stopping the wagon train to ask some Indian the way to California?

Resolution #3. — *The toilet seat controversy.* Toilet seat positioning is optional, but the up position is preferred out of consideration for those whose first priority is a clean bowl. The up position facilitates inspection.

Resolution #4. — *The "fix it" syndrome.* Men should listen carefully when people describe their problems and not automatically offer to fix things. People usually just want to be heard and supported. Certainly it takes will power to fight the urge to solve the problem, but an enlightened man will persevere. A case in point: One World Congress member proudly told of coming upon a car with a flat tire parked along a remote stretch of highway. An immaculately dressed business woman jumped out of the car and lamented that she was late for a chance-of-a-lifetime job interview. "So," drawled our enlightened hero, "How does that make you feel?"

Resolution #5. — *Feelings.* A motion calling upon men to discuss their feelings was tabled indefinitely.

Women Talk

As I was walking with two women a while ago, one asked me a question. Then, in the midst of my answer, she gestured toward a house and said, "So that's why they painted the shutters pink. They match the roses in the front yard."

I saw her interruption as a sure sign of a short attention span and stopped talking. I also made a mental note to shrug more in her presence and to give brief answers — like "yep," "nope," and "don't know."

Although it's been very educational to read Deborah Tannen's and John Gray's best sellers about the different ways men and women communicate, for me the most useful information came during an informal front porch discussion at a friend's beach house. The topic was male/female talk patterns. It was, actually, a bit humbling to realize that half of western civilization (the female half) has always known what I just found out during that discussion: that women can actually hear what is being said when several of them are talking simultaneously.

I've noticed the multiple talk process for a long time. And I sensed that the participants were enjoying it. But it never occurred to me that they were actually following what was being said. I always thought group talk was just a ritual; sort of the female counterpart to Tarzan's chest thumping jungle whoop — that it was important as a social rite, but that no one actually gleaned information from it.

Now I understand women's propensity to talk ensemble is something more. They actually know what's being said. And it's not just that women have a superior intellect which enables them to understand that which is a cacophony to my gender, as one woman wryly suggested. Other women in our conversation smiled knowingly and said, "Yes, we hear it all." I have asked individual women who were not in the discussion if they hear it all. They said yes. *All* of them said yes. For me, that revelation was astounding — a little like discovering I was the only one in the room who couldn't levitate.

According to Tannen, PhD and Gray, PhD, women have a distinctive conversational style when they are among themselves. And so do men. When the genders are mixed, men and women talk in yet another way — a way that is neither men talk nor women talk (but closer to men talk.) When just one man is in a conversation with two or more women, they very often talk women's style.

Armed with my new knowledge, I see my walk with the two women differently now. The woman who interrupted me, apparently forgetting for the moment my innate male handicap, probably thought it was a male idiosyncrasy (or a sure sign of a short attention span), that I stopped talking halfway through my answer.

Fear

In case you didn't know, men don't "fear" anything. At least, they don't call it that. They may be skeptical or leery of those aspects of the coupling process, for instance, that are risky. But they (we) don't admit to being scared.

That all became abundantly clear the other night at the discussion of a book called, "He's Scared, She's Scared," in which the capacity group (complete with waiting list) included only three men. There were so few men there because men don't read books with titles that are so obviously flawed. The meeting would have had a better gender balance if it had been called "She's Scared, He's Reviewing the Situation."

If men sometimes fail to commit, as the book the meeting was based on suggests, it's because they have a darned good reason. They are not scared. It's just that they like to keep their options open. Or they're still weighing the pros and cons. Or they fully intend to commit but not now. After all, it would be pointless for a man to commit before his lease runs out. Besides, there are tax, pension and inheritance questions to be considered. Whatever the reason, it has nothing to do with fear and lets not talk about it now.

We men come by this awesome valor honestly. In our lives,

we've had countless examples to emulate. Think of our great role model of the 30s, 40s, 50s, 60s and 70s, John Wayne. He didn't know the meaning of fear. Would the wagons ever have gotten to the West if John Wayne had been scared? Heck no. They'd probably still be circling somewhere in Ohio.

At that meeting, I volunteered that I was put off by women who declare to the world how "independent" they are now that they are single. Too often that has meant they have become totally self-involved and difficult to get along with. The facilitator summed up with "John fears women who say they are independent."

It was, of course, necessary for me to remind her that men do not fear, they merely become discerning. The remaining man in the discussion agreed with me. (The third guy had already left because the hostess's cat was wreaking havoc with his allergies His leave-taking was motivated, of course, by prudence, not fear.)

That meeting was proof positive that men don't come to discussions that might characterize them as "scared." Or, maybe the reason they didn't come is they're slow to sign up. In fact, it's a proven, scientific fact that men wait till the last minute to sign up for virtually everything. And this meeting was so good, it filled up early. Come to think of it, I'll bet that's the whole reason there were so few men there.

These hairy-chested guys aren't afraid to discuss fear. They're just slow to commit — even to a week-night discussion packed with lovely single women.

Eye Contact

"Yoohoo, I'm over here" said the sweet young thing as I looked around the room, at the waitress, at the restaurant decor, the menu, a glass of water, the floor, the ceiling and over her shoulder but seldom directly at her. She couldn't understand why I had such trouble looking into her eyes. Actually, I didn't either.

But I do now: For a man, making eye contact — actually locking one's eyes on another — is aggressive and confrontational. For a woman, it's a way of establishing rapport.

You think I'm making this up?

Here are some cases in point:

— When a father is scolding his son, the father makes eye contact, but the son doesn't.

— Deborah Tannen, the savvy author of "You Just Don't Understand," asked two pre-teen girls to wait in a room with two chairs. They turned the chairs toward each other and chatted idly. Next, she put two pre-teen boys in the same room with the same chairs. Predictably, they turned their chairs toward the window and chatted without looking at each other.

— When men are having sex, they look their women in the eye. Probably. Actually I've never seen a man and woman having sex. But I'll bet it's universally true that aroused men have no trouble looking their women in the eye.

— Neither do angry men. If it's really that important that a woman's date look into her eyes, she need only do something outrageous to make him very angry. She might try telling him he's a thief, a liar, a sleaze and a pedophile. That ought to do it.

— Men bent on criminal acts look their victims in the eye, albeit sometimes through a ski mask. If they weren't in such a hurry, purse snatchers probably would too.

Averting one's eyes is an old ploy steeped in history, nature and even national security. Sometimes it's used to avoid alerting a potential adversary. Some examples

— The marquee at the Marriott Hotel announced that the vice president was scheduled to speak. The red carpet had already been rolled out. A few secret service men lolled about paying no attention to me or the satchel I was carrying through the lobby on my way to work-out at the adjoining National Press Club. I was not impressed by their vigilance - - until a few minutes later as I was changing into my sweats. The dressing room door swung open and one of the Secret Service agents glanced at me, then, apparently satisfied, disappeared. He had followed me. The two secret service agents purposely had avoided eye contact with me in the lobby.

— The lion sits at the edge of the savanna as a herd of tasty gazelles whiz on by. He doesn't look at them; just sits there licking his paws -- or whatever lions do to look preoccupied. The gazelles let down their guards. "Must not be meal time," they probably think. Then, pow, the lion strikes.

— Monte Roberts, author of "The Man Who Listens to Horses" and the inspiration for the Robert Redford movie "The Horse Whisperer," says he gains a horse's trust in large part by pointedly not looking him in the eye.

Well it's all been a lesson to me. When I was a kid, we thought the reason people didn't look you in the eye was because they were lying. If they wanted to prove otherwise, they had to look you in the eye and say George Washington three times without smiling.

Like all good rules, of course, there are exceptions. For a long time, I wondered what magic my old beach-house buddy Josh performed that drew women to him. He was sure he had some sort of animal magnetism. I wasn't convinced. In fact, although I liked him personally, I thought his behavior with women was downright sleazy. But I couldn't deny that women were drawn to him.

Years later, I came across a passage in a book on body language that described an exception to the men-avert-their-eyes rule: a man who stares at women, even strangers — especially strangers. Since women have no trouble making eye contact, they return his gaze. And the dance of romance begins.

I asked a woman friend if it was not a bit disconcerting to have a strange man stare at her from across the room. I thought she'd say it would raise a yellow flag of caution. Instead she said she'd love it; she'd think he was so taken with her that he just couldn't take his eyes off her. She'd want to get to know him.

So much for Josh's animal magnetism. I rest my case.

Burdenless

Men can't really understand how overwhelming it is to be a single, custodial mother with a job and an attempted social life, a woman friend told me recently. She said it's a special anguish that bonds women together. And even the most caring man hasn't a clue what it's like.

I'm sure she didn't mean to slight custodial fathers and women without children. They have their own special burdens. Nevertheless, I was interested in her comment because she's certainly right about me.

Since I've been single again, all four of my children have lived with me at one time or another. — and four of my grandchildren have. Yet, married or single, I was never in charge of getting their suppers ready. If one of them caught a cold, I went to work anyway. I didn't have to help them with homework or pack their lunches. I was only vaguely aware of the condition of their clothes (which they washed themselves.) I didn't have to arrange sleep-overs or find baby sitters or change their bedding.

But women routinely perform those tasks. The women at the recent "Men Are From Mars..." book discussion lamented that they sometimes feel overwhelmed. I mentioned that I could not remember feeling overwhelmed and they looked at me as if I were from Mars....which, given the topic of the discussion, I suppose, was appropriate.

I wonder what men's burdens might be — other than a seemingly innate inability to identify their burdens. Oh sure, we feel a crushing responsibility to be good providers, to secure the well-being of our families, and to set a good example. But who doesn't?

We also are called upon to fight wars, fix flat tires, carve Thanksgiving turkeys, and take out the trash. Whereas fighting wars is certainly burdensome, it's also fairly rare. I was in the army myself, but I never fought a war. Don't think I would have cared for it much. But those other things — turkeys, tires and trash — can hardly be considered burdens.

Okay you guys, we need a burden. Preferably one that women won't understand. Male burdens must exist somewhere or life would be easier and we men would be having more fun.

Shopping

Let's examine the phenomenon of shopping — a time-honored tradition about which many contemporary single men (like me) haven't a clue. Married men may know.

To me, and I suppose many men who live alone, there are only three types of shopping: Food, Product and Christmas.

Food shopping is simple. When you run out of milk, you go to the supermarket to get some more. And while you're there, you pick up some bread and cold meat. Maybe some eggs, butter, mayonnaise, a few boxes of Raisin Nut Bran and anything else that you've run out of or soon will. If you forget anything, that's okay, you'll be back in a few days to get more milk. You can pick it up then.

Product shopping includes buying a new car, or a new suit, or a new pair of shoes. Those things break down, wear out, and go out of style. But just plain "shopping" without the word "for" after it, seems like an incomplete sentence.

In December, one goes into huge, crowded malls, chooses articles one would never buy under normal circumstances and gives them away to other people -- especially children. That's Christmas shopping. It's a hassle, but it doesn't last long and makes children happy. So we do it year after year.

But you already know all that.

What you may not know, especially if you are a single man, is that those same cavernous structures that you traverse during the jolly season are used during the off-season in a pervasive recreational activity called simply "shopping." It's sort of a group-participation sport -- a mix of fox hunting, arm wrestling, and running with the bulls.

Shopping must be connected to nurturing somehow because all the truly dedicated shoppers seem to be women. I've never heard a man say, for instance, "Let's meet downtown for lunch, and then go shopping," or "I'm so tired, I spent all day shopping."

Out-of-town trade conventions typically invite members to bring their spouses who are encouraged to "shop" while the members attend business meetings. (That may be changing as more women join the members ranks.)

Its adherents say shopping is fun, but by no means frivolous. I'm told it is what makes America great. It supports the economy, and keeps the country's mills, factories and shopping centers churning out new products. And the bootie from countless shopping sprees nationwide ultimately beautifies homes and enriches citizens from Maine to Hawaii. It makes a core contribution to the American way of life. It's selfless and it's patriotic -- a 21st century counterpart to Rosie the Riveter and U.S. Savings Bonds.

I interviewed a random sample of shoppers to get some insights. Here's what I learned:

1. Women tend to shop in groups of two or more -- probably a variation on their propensity for visiting the ladies' room in pairs.

2. Shopping often includes lunch.

3. Shopping is systematic. One tours the whole store carefully examining and discussing multiple items.

4. One compares prices between stores and often goes back to get the best bargain.

5. Shoppers seldom ask directions in department stores because they already know where everything is.

6. Shoppers do a good deal of "impulse buying." They see no need to justify their purchases to themselves or anyone else because they can always return them.

7. Shoppers return many of their purchases. And while they're there, they shop for more. (Don't knock it, it's a system that works.)

I took a short-cut through a department store with a woman colleague who I suspect is a closet shopper. She kept fingering things and turning them over as we walked by. "Those draperies would look good on my dining room windows," she muttered in the midst of our discussion of international trade sanctions. Well, I've seen her dining room windows. They already have curtains. Nice ones. What would ever possess her to buy a second set?

I mentioned the incident to a very savvy woman friend. "Of course she's a shopper," she said. "Every woman is. How did you think those stores were used after you've finished your Christmas shopping?"

"Well, I thought, you know, if someone needed to buy a shirt, for instance, during the off season, it'd be nice to have a fully staffed Neiman-Marcus there..." I could see the flaw in my rationale even before I ever finished my sentence. And she was decidedly less impressed when I told her I often shop on the Internet.

"That's not shopping," she snapped, "that's ordering."

Too Fussy

I **get so tired of hearing women** complain that there are no good single men out there. If you ask me, women are too fussy. They find one little fault in a man, then obsess about it.

As a case in point, I put together descriptions and phone numbers for seven men at random — men who are really very nice once you get to know them. And best of all, ladies, they'd love to meet you. Feel free to call:

Reggie "Blunt" Instrument, 307-427-2131, 51 years old, imaginative, unpredictable, loves a good time, powerful physique, not presently involved, complains that he has no way of meeting like-minded women — or any women. A fun guy. (Leave a message with the warden and Blunt will get back to you during his regular weekly phone-usage hour.)

Alvin Paniwaist, 229-304-7677, a nice looking guy, 46 years old, intelligent, financially secure, never been married, heterosexual, lives with his mother, no bad habits. (Plan something during the day — his mother doesn't let him go out after dark.)

Frank A. Sault, 499-234-0928, 43, says he knows how to treat a woman, long-time boyfriend of the late Ann Battery.

128. - Single Over Thirty

Due to a tragic childhood, this poor man needs love and understanding and tends to lose his temper if he doesn't get it — as Ann could attest if she were still around.

Grub Grunch, 222-233-4456, 50-ish, very relaxed, not a worrier. No job, no money, no skills, no friends, no problems. Doesn't bathe. Loves pro wrestling. Hates shoes. A real diamond in the rough. Think of him as clay just waiting to be kneaded into someone spectacular.

Ronnie "Romeo" Romano, 267-094-3921, 49, says there's something about him women can't resist. Often has two or three dates in the same evening. Drives a bright red Porsche convertible. His cell phone rings constantly. Loves women but has a hard time remembering their names. Needs to know if you are an early evening persons or a late evening person. Your place or his?

Lush Lundigan, 948-549-0030, 44, says he drives better when he's drunk. A great, fun date when he remembers to show up. Doesn't recall ever having been mean or unkind when he's been drinking. Doesn't remember much at all about such times. Has famous friends. On a first name basis with Betty Ford who refers to him affectionately as "you again."

Alfred D. Crepid, 230-432-0096, 79 (or so), loves younger women, likes to sit or lie down, drives slowly with his turn signal always blinking, tells stories endlessly, knows everything, wears too much after shave, can't hear you.

Well, that was fun. Now I'd like to put together a similar list of women.

But I can't. Those men are scary. Women seldom are. Although there are infrequent exceptions to the rule, women generally are not aggressive, don't beat-up smaller people, don't go to prison, don't bird-dog men half their ages, and don't live with their fathers.

Women alcoholics are seldom as public about it as men are. And although they may be unfaithful in the same numbers as men, they are seldom the aggressors and, no matter how monied, they almost never drive bright red Porsche convertibles.

So what obnoxious things do women do that men don't?

For one thing, they leave their pantihose hanging in the bathroom. Give me some time. I'll think of more.

Choice

Who really makes the first move? Men or women? I was in a divided discussion the other day in which one side said the women really made the choices of romantic partners and the men only thought they did.

The other side said men, being the aggressive ones, made the choices, showed initial interest, asked for the first date, asked for a dance, made follow-up phone calls, sent flowers and pursued. And women, ever the hopeful romantics, rationalize that anyone who has clean fingernails and goes to all that trouble must indeed be a good match.

My friend Orme, a typical man, thinks he chooses. He has a sort of a free-floating, potential romantic interest in a whole lot of women simultaneously. Most of them, of course, are beyond his reach. They tend to be movie actresses, international models, stars of their own TV series, or celebrities featured on the cover of Newsweek. He's never met them. But in the unlikely event that he found himself at a swanky party populated by those women, and one of them looked his way, smiled and winked, Orme would still think he, not she, had made the choice. He would not bat his eyelashes, smile demurely, blush and look at the floor waiting for her to follow up.

More likely he'd claw and trample his way across the room to where she was standing and introduce himself.

I know this scenario of Orme choosing from a menu of beautiful luminaries is a bit of a stretch, but stay with me. I'm enjoying it vicariously.

From her viewpoint, the woman would probably think she made the first move. She might reason that, had she not winked and smiled, nothing would have happened. No one would have been clawed or trampled because Orme would not have been motivated to move post haste to her side. And as far as that goes, she's right. What she doesn't realize is that Orme had already made a choice -- in fact several. All her wink did was create in Orme a sudden mental imbalance. Predictable and no big deal.

If all men were blessed with cast iron egos, unrelenting self confidence, and foot-thick skin, they'd need no such encouragement.

Any man might approach any woman at any time. What the heck. It'd be sort of a free lottery. Everything to gain, nothing to lose.

But, sadly, men have egos that bruise. They go to great lengths to avoid being humiliated, embarrassed, diminished, ridiculed, or told the truth. And they're especially averse to brawling with irate husbands and boyfriends. So they approach with caution or not at all.

Also, it's a scientific fact that men are attracted to women by criteria far more complex and enduring than mere pulchritude. They really are. Honest. Some of them.

Sasha has a differing view. She thinks women make the first move by showing an interest in and encouraging the object of their choices.

"If he catches me looking at him a few times during the evening, he'll surely come over to say hello," she says. "If he doesn't, there's probably a good reason. He's spoken for, gay, or I'm just not his cup of tea."

If, after a time, the relationship fails, incredibly, women like Sasha tend to ask "Why do I keep choosing the wrong men?" That's probably when she is most convinced that she made the choice and that she made it poorly.

Men, it seems to me, have no such second thoughts about their judgement. "It's over. Not my fault."

Certainly both don't make the choice at the same time. Only in works of fiction do sparks fly in both directions simultaneously at the initial meeting. But in the real world, somebody makes the first move. Either the man or the woman acts. And the other reacts.

So who really makes the first move? I'm convinced that men do.

Except sometimes.

It's a little like fishing, isn't it? Men make the choice in that they are ever trolling. And women decide, based on how much they are attracted to the fisherman, whether to take the bait.

Or is it the women who do the trolling?

Fantasy

Sometimes I wish life were more like it is in HBO's "Sex and the City," a weekly TV show that pushes the envelope a bit. It's the continuing story of four successful 30-something New York career women who are very candid about their up-scale sex lives. The key scenes are usually situational and conversational; very rarely explicitly visual.

One exception was an episode in which the four attended an oh-so-chic, in-crowd, dazzling, daring cocktail party. A cocktail waitress circulated about the floor carrying a tray of drinks at shoulder height. Guests smiled at the waitress admiringly as they deposited their empty glasses on the tray and picked up full ones. The waitress seemed to pay no attention. She was wearing high heels and a gold bracelet. And that's all.

Frankly, I found it rather titillating in an it'd-never-happen sort of way. I later told the woman I was dating about it. She didn't smile.

"I'd have left that party immediately and cut off the people who threw it from my life forever," she said.

"Whoa. Come on. It's just a fantasy. Make believe." I was

a bit disappointed. Where was her sense of the bizarre? I hadn't really thought beyond make-believe. Apparently my date had. So I decided to think about how I would respond if it had *really* happened. To me.

What if I had gone to an ever-so-chic party and the cocktail waitress was beautiful and naked.

Assuming I wasn't there with the woman who wanted to leave immediately, I think I'd have several reactions that were different in real life than they were in fantasy. My first reaction would be embarrassment for the naked lady. And sympathy. I would not automatically assume she was a hooker. A little kookie, perhaps, and certainly daring, but most likely doing it for the money. To me, that would mean some low-life was taking advantage of her need for money by making her do something demeaning. A bully with deep pockets. Not my favorite kind of person.

Secondly, I would fear for her safety. The likelihood that she could parade a gorgeous naked body through a floor crowded with gin-guzzling strangers and not get groped, grabbed, pinched, goosed, humiliated, stroked, insulted, or propositioned seemed slim.

And finally, I think I'd have some fear for my date and myself. This is an unstable situation. The people in charge made some very flaky decisions. Who knows what kind of activity follows this one? I don't think I would necessarily get my coat and bolt, but I might stand near the door and be very alert to any sign of escalation. And if I saw it, then I might very well bolt.

Otherwise, for the rest of the evening I'd be aware at all times exactly where the naked woman was. It would be difficult to resist shooting furtive glances in her direction. I'm sure my date would notice this and not be pleased. I'd enjoy watching the waitress and I'd have a suppressed desire to get to know her — but, don't worry, I wouldn't act on it in a million years.

I'd probably think twice before attending any other parties thrown by the same cadre of revelers. After all, there are safer places to ogle beautiful naked women, if that is one's desire. Still, I'd gleefully debrief those who had attended and enjoy their accounts vicariously -- just as I had enjoyed the scene on Sex and the City.

Has anything like that ever really happened? Probably lots of times, but I only know of one. And it turned out badly.

During the Roaring 20s, Earl Carroll, an obscenely rich and successful Broadway producer, threw a no-expense-spared all-night party back stage for a very select, if somewhat decadent, group of New York insiders. To spice up the party, he hired a teen-aged model to take a champagne bath in a tub set up on stage.

Then male guests lined up, champagne glasses in hand, and scooped drinks out of the tub. The naked teenager began to cry in embarrassment. Party goers, decadent or not, were so outraged at the poor girl's humiliation, they covered her and got her home. Many left the party early. The press got wind of the story, the mogul was disgraced and, 80 years later, people like me are still telling the story.

An afterthought: What if instead of the real-life party, the mogul had made a movie that included a similar champagne-bath scene, and used a seasoned actress to play the teenager? Wouldn't the fantasy be acceptable?

Nah, my date still would have walked out of the theater.

Libido

Libido is a Latin word. It means desire. Actually, the way we use it today, it means burning sexual desire. You probably know for sure whether you have it. And you probably know for sure when your partner doesn't.

I grew up thinking that only men had libidos. I thought women were simply being accommodating and, even then, only occasionally. And before she would accommodate her man, in my youthful view, a woman had to expect that something valuable might come of their coupling; something like returned love, security, warmth, support, money, power, a family, stability, or good times. In that sense, I thought, women probably had libidos too. But libido in the powerful, compelling sense that I experienced it? Dream on.

My view has changed, of course. I watch television. I see the cover of Cosmopolitan on newsstands. I hear women proclaim that certain men have "tight butts." But my old mental set still haunts me for several reasons:

1. Although I only know my own libido intimately, it's no great stretch for me to understand other men's. But I have no inkling of women's libidos. The things that turn them on are the very things that turn me off. Probably. I'm not that sure what turns them on. And, no doubt, it's just as well. Certainly if I knew, I'd be tempted to take unfair advantage of my insider information.

2. I don't see clear signs of women's libidos the way I see men's. What little I detect is so subtle, so strategic, so obscured beneath the folds. In most romantic pursuits, man is the aggressor. He and his libido get things started. If a woman's interest is peaked before a man's — it could happen — one might not recognize it immediately. Her strategy is more likely to subtly focus his libido on her. By contrast, a man in his libido mode is more likely to pull out all the stops and launch into full, reckless pursuit. Batten down the hatches. Damn the torpedoes. Full steam ahead. Get out of my way.

(The above points may be sociologically invalid, but humor me.)

Libidos don't simply erupt spontaneously in pairs. For coupling to work, somebody has to get it started and draw the other in. It's very important that person #2 responds to person #1's display of libido. Picture the scene if that were not so. Joe would chase Jane who would chase Harold who would chase Alexandra who would chase Bob and on and on. Well, yeah, right. That's the way it often is now. But it would be more so. At some point, someone has to turn his/her libido onto the person whose libido is focused on them. Otherwise it would be musical beds. Well, yeah, I know. It sometimes is anyway. But not nearly as much as if libido didn't respond to libido.

Okay, now it's starting to make a little more sense.

Libido certainly isn't the only reason people fall in love. There are myriad other highly complex reasons. Libido simply jump-starts the process. If libido were the only criteria, our civilization might look like the ribald fields of Woodstock during the 1969 rock concert. On the other hand, without libido, it might look like Woodstock four days later when it was a sprawl of barren ground, trampled vegetation and wind-blown litter.

Life Is a Dance Floor

At dances, I don't have much of a feel for what it is about men that initially attracts women. Perhaps it's enough that they're handsome and that they come up and say hello. More likely, it's something I would never understand anyway.

Nor do I know what initially attracts my fellow males to certain women and not to others. But I do know what attracts me. And here it is:

Step 1 *(We meet.)* From across a crowded dance floor with the lights down low, I can't tell whether a woman has a great personality, sterling character, intelligence, talent, ethics, or depth. So, shallow rascal that I am, I am attracted by her appearance.

I am most likely to focus on a woman who is slim to normal — sometimes a teeny bit beyond normal girth. I am intrigued by a sense of style, the right combination of clothes and jewelry. I revel in clean with a light scent of perfume. I am drawn by pretty faces that wear pleasant expressions and slightly understated makeup. I groove on women who are a little animated, who smile and move easily. The smile suggests they are pleasant; the movement, that they are active and in good health.

(Granted, women like that don't always fancy me back, but that's not what we're talking about here, is it?)

Step 2 *(We dance.)* I don't care if she's a good dancer. Dances are not so much about dancing as they are about getting to know each other.

Step 3 *(We talk... except sometimes.)* I danced with a woman once who said nothing during the dance and the instant it was over did a military about-face, then marched briskly away.

That was probably my shortest-ever relationship. Usually we talk. And that's how she and I get to know each other.

Even when it isn't on a dance floor, sight has a lot to do with the initial interest for me (and, I suspect, for most men). It's so safe. By surreptitiously scanning the far side of the room, one can start the selection process without alerting any of the prospective candidates. (Try doing that with conversation.)

That's how it has always been for me — until now, of course. Nowadays I first get to know people from the safety and comfort of singles events, discussions, weekends excursions, and other group social events. Participating in such activities takes far less cheek than walking up to a perfect stranger at a dance and asking her if I can hold her body against mine to the beat of some pretty suggestive music.

Part of the reason for my (former) intrigue with mere physical beauty has been the brainwashing I got from the songs and poetry I grew up with. I'd be a better man today if, for instance, Irving Berlin had written "*A Pleasant Personality Is Like a Melody,*" and Stephen Foster, "*Intelligent Dreamer.*" ... and if Christopher Marlowe had immortalized Helen of Troy more appropriately as "*...the strength of character that launched a thousand ships.*"

Crying

There's a scene in the movie, "Moonstruck," where the Cher character's boyfriend is bemoaning his fate and Cher has an immediate solution to his dilemma. She slaps him in the face and says, "Snap out of it."

In real life, you can't do that. When someone moans or, Lord forbid, cries out loud, you are duty-bound to be sympathetic. It doesn't matter if you know the answers to their problems, you must speak in low, soothing tones.

If the crier is a woman and you are a man, you must give her a hug, kiss the top of her head, pat her back gently and say words to the effect of, "There-there. It's okay."

That's not fair. Women cry a lot more than men do. So men end up being the comforter, the nurturer. The nurturer? I thought women were supposed to be the nurturers and men were the providers.

It's not their fault, of course. Women just cry when they feel like it. There's noting wrong with that. Men, on the other hand, fight the urge with a vengeance. Crying for women is an expression of temporary emotional imbalance (TEI). They even cry sometimes when they're happy.

At moments of TEI, men are more likely to become silent, turn away, change the subject, watch TV, tell a joke, or leave. On rare occasions, you might see moisture well up in their eyes. But you've got to be quick.

Women are so up-front about crying, they typically mention it in casual conversation. "I was so upset, I cried."

Men would never do that. First, they probably wouldn't cry. They might shout, or swear, or read someone the riot act, or threaten, or gnash their teeth. But they wouldn't cry. And if they ever did, they surely wouldn't tell anyone about it.

When a woman cries, it tends to upset the man she's with. In those rare moments when a man cries in public, it upsets everyone on down the block and probably several people in the next town. Women are supposed to cry. It's their way of dealing. Men aren't supposed to cry. It's a rule.

John Wayne made more than 200 movies over a 50 year period and never cried once. Conversely, the most accomplished actresses routinely cry in their best Oscar-winning performances. In fact, that may be how they won the Oscar: Because they cry so well.

Okay, now I think I've made the point that women cry easily and men don't and that it's nobody's fault -- just the way things are. As far as I know, it's not a cultural thing. I know of no foreign lands in which the roles are reversed. Women cry all round the globe. And men try not to. (Granted, some try harder than others.)

Normally, when people cry, it's not a pretty picture. First, it sounds bad. It's not the "whaa" or "sob" sound featured in books and cartoon strips. It's a hoarse, coughing, gasping, gagging, honking, out-of-control sound. And the crier's appearance changes from beautiful to blotchy. Eyes turn red and watery. The nose runs. And the face screws up into a grimace.

But it can have its compensations. When women cry and men comfort them, men get a real sense of closeness and being needed. There is something so elemental about having a lovely, warm, soft woman clinging desperately to one, her scented hair gathered fragrantly beneath one's nose. So feminine and so like a perfumed garden.

I don't know what men's hair smells like. Probably Vaseline.

Cup of Tea

Josh asked Betty to join him and a group of his friends two-weeks hence on a Sunday afternoon and she responded simply, "Sorry, I have previous plans," and nothing more. No other details. No "but keep me in mind if you do this sort of thing again," nor any other words that suggest she'd prefer his company to a root canal.

Josh interpreted that unforthcoming reply as a message. And that message is "Josh, you're just not my cup of tea." Well, that's okay. Between you and me, Josh isn't everyone's cup of tea. And he knows it. His feelings weren't hurt, but he was taken-back by his own mis-reading of her interest. Whatever. Josh won't ask her out again. And that's that.

That all seems like a reasonable scenario to me -- a painless way of being rejected. She doesn't exhibit any interest. He won't ask her out again. She doesn't have to make up convoluted excuses. He doesn't feel rejected.

A casual friendship remains in tact. But what if Josh is wrong? What if there was no real significance to her response? As Freud said, sometimes a cigar is just a cigar. This reading signs is tricky business. It assumes you're both on the same page, that you read these subtle little messages the same.

What if she doesn't read the scenario the way Josh does? What if she fully expects he'll ask her out again? What if the day in question is the date of a mutual friend's wedding and Betty was invited but Josh wasn't? What if Betty just woke up from a nap and wasn't her usual perky self? Or perhaps she didn't want to seem too anxious. Maybe sending and receiving subtle messages is not her strong suit. Maybe she just has a laid-back personality.

So, if Josh's technique is the wrong one, what's the right one? Don't say that they should be totally honest with each other. The whole purpose of this coded communication is to avoid honesty. Total, brutal honesty could be deadly. Here's a sample:

Josh: "Hi Betty, it's Josh. I'd like to start a process with you that hopefully will end in my bed. Can you join me and my friends etc. etc."

Betty: "Lucky for me, I have plans to go to a Patty's wedding that day. Obviously you weren't invited. Also, the thought of being a couple with you makes me nauseous. Further, I don't like you for the following reasons etc. etc."

Okay, total honesty is out of the question. How about a sort of abbreviated honesty in which Josh persists by asking her if she'd like to go to a movie or dinner at some other time? And she says either yes or no.

If she says no, he would surely feel rejected and their hitherto casual friendship would suffer strain. If she says yes, they've saved what might be a successful coupling - or at least an enjoyable dinner date. She also might mumble, "Yeah, sure, whatever." This is not an expression of enthusiasm. I would hope Josh might never quite get around to asking her again. But, knowing ever-hopeful Josh, he probably would.

Hero

All **the fuss over whether** Pfc. Jessica Lynch was a bona fide hero or just a contrived poster child for the Iraq war has made me think about what a hero really is.

The dictionary says a hero is a man who is big, strong, courageous and favored by the gods. That doesn't fit petite, 19-year-old Pfc. Jessica Lynch.

The second definition says it's a man noted for his feats of courage and nobility of purpose, especially one who has risked or sacrificed his life. If you've seen photos of her, you know that Jessica Lynch is definitely not a man, although she may be noble and courageous, but by her own words, sacrificing her life was what she was trying not to do.

The third definition (there were six) is one who is prominent in "his" discipline. Still not a "his" and, as an army Private First Class, Lynch probably was not actually prominent in the same sense that Eisenhower, for instance, was. I was a Pfc. myself and I never had the feeling I was regarded as prominent by the Pentagon.

Scratch also No. 4, the male lead character in a novel and, No.5., a potential lover or protector. Neither fits Jessica.

So that leaves us with definition No. 6, a huge sandwich. aka a hoagie, a sub, and a grinder.

I rest my case.

So why do I -- and so many other people -- admire her so?

I'm sure this makes me a sexist and maybe a Neanderthal, but personally, I value her because she is a pretty young woman who miraculously survived a bleak predicament, in a patriotic (to the U.S.) cause, with honesty, modesty and humility. And, I suppose, because I have the protective mind-set of a father of two daughters, and because she reminds me of every pretty girl I admired in high school. I like her too because she said, "I am a soldier too" to her captors, which I thought was gutsy, loyal and even cute. If she were a man, I hope her rescuers still would have made the effort. But, let's face it, a rescued male soldier wouldn't have made the cover of Time magazine. No interview by Diane Sawyer. No massive home town celebration. No made-for-TV movie. And no best selling book.

We men -- some of us -- fantasize that women are precious beings to be cherished, protected and defended. The act of plucking such a sweet young thing out of the jaws of a cruel war, from behind enemy lines, is enormously appealing. But it doesn't make her a hero.

The men who saved her were the heroes (see the definitions above.) She was the prize that made the success of their rescue mission so stunning that it fired the emotions of a nation.

Having said all that, there are two dictionary definitions for the word "heroine." The first is the female lead character in a drama. The second is simply the female counterpart of a hero.

The dictionary makes no mention of a heroine sandwich.

Men and Women

Everybody knows that men have beards and don't ask for directions, and that women seldom go bald and visit the ladies room in pairs. But what are some of the more subtle differences?

I put that question to some friends at a weekend retreat and was gratified at the differences they identified and just a bit disappointed that some of them saw the differences as a failure of the other gender. To me that explains much of the anger and misunderstanding that triggers breakups.

So think of this column as a public service. These are the things that aren't anyone's fault. For the sake of peace between the sexes, assume they are innate traits that have evolved over the eons to make the coupling process work -- assuming of course that it does. Also note that the following observations are the work of amateurs. They are rank generalizations. I hope you'll be skeptical of some of them. I certainly am.

To begin, men and women move differently. It's difficult to define the difference, but from several city blocks away, one can usually identify a person's gender by the way they walk. Women are more graceful in their movements. Men move more heavily and deliberately. Except sometimes.

Women are more perceptive in group situations, one woman observed. They sense others' moods and attitudes better than men do, but men, she said, are more attuned to visual surroundings. Never mind that our hostess put flowers in everyone's room, and my roommate and I didn't notice ours until the third day.

Women are more likely to let themselves be vulnerable in a relationship men are more guarded about expressing their feelings.

Men, spit with impunity. While 10 million television viewers look on, a major league pitcher thinks nothing of letting go of a hawker before he lets go of the ball. Women seldom spit and they readily express their disdain for the men who do -- which has led to an epidemic of spitting on the sly. What women do with their spittle remains one of life's deepest mysteries.

Most men lack women's style and finesse, as their bachelor quarters typically demonstrate. Some may even show up for dates unshaven and in Bermuda shorts, sneakers and baseball caps. Women are natural beautifiers. They dress well, clean up after themselves, wear make up, have their hair done, and generally have style.

Men "report talk," saying what needs to be said then stopping while women "rapport talk," trying to put people at ease, making friends, spreading cheer.

Men are pragmatic, they want to fix things. Women are supportive. They want everyone to feel good and be happy.

Men are bigger, stronger and more aggressive. Women are more graceful, gentle and tend to be more conciliatory.

Women's voices are higher, men's deeper -- but you've

probably already noticed that.

Men are hairier, except on their heads where they'd really rather have all that extra hair.

Men have more solid handshakes. Mostly.

Men are more erotically turned-on by what they see. Women are more tactile.

Men can be dangerous, women seldom are. Men commit crimes and go to jail in great numbers. Women don't. Nobody worries about meeting a female stranger in a dark ally.

Women cry, men don't. One woman in our group said in her lifetime, she only saw a man cry once. And it was unnerving.

One man may put-down another by telling him he throws a ball or runs like a girl. Women seldom denigrate members of their own gender by comparing them to a boy.

Women look people in the eye when they talk. And they go to the ladies room in pairs. Men stare elsewhere when they talk and would rather go to the men's room alone, thanks.

Women's aggression toward each other is almost never physical, but when angered, they go into a snit, deliberately distancing themselves from the other. Although men seldom come to blows (one can get hurt that way), they are more direct and threatening when angered.

Women give (and would like to receive) many small, meaningful gifts. Men give infrequent but more elaborate gifts. They don't think much about receiving unexpected gifts themselves.

Women need reassurance. Men need reassurance more explicitly. That means women need to get a hug and a kiss to feel loved. Men need to hear the words.

Men compartmentalize, concentrating their full energies on the task at hand. Women multi-task. That is, they might simultaneously be thinking of their jobs, what to make for supper, and their boyfriends -- all at the same time. And, of course, they're a bit frustrated with boyfriends who don't call during the day just to tell her they're thinking about her.

Women can give each other a peck on the lips without grossing out bystanders. Men better not try.

Extra weight goes to men's stomachs, to women's hips.

Women wear make-up, high heels and sparkling jewelry. Men don't, usually.

Women go shopping. Most men don't fully understand the phenomenon.

Some men dig gross humor. Women think it's gross. And, of course, it is. That's what makes it so funny. To men.

Women are more hygienic than men. A woman with body odor is a rarity. A man is not.

Coupled women say they fall heir to the role of social chairman and they don't like it. When that task is left to men, they tend not make plans in any detail -- if at all.

Women are more conscious of whether they are perceived as a couple. Men seem to be on the prowl.

A woman can send a card with a humorous sexual innuendo to a man and it's considered to be funny and a bit daring. But if a man sends a woman such a card, it's considered to be a clumsy, course advance.

Men work together better than women do.

Women feel slighted more easily than men.

Women routinely use words like adorable, lovely, precious and cute. Men don't. (One woman in our group balked, opining that the only word men are reluctant to use is "commitment.")

Women know each other better than men do because they converse more and talk about personal subjects like problems and feelings. Men don't and therefore don't know each other or women as well.

The exchange of good natured insults is a bonding mechanism for men. But not so for women who bond by validating each other. Women who have been insulted, good-naturedly or not, are not amused.

Rob Becker in his one-man show, "Defending the Caveman," gives an example of differing styles when two couples get together for the first time in years. The two women compliment each other on their clothes, hairstyles and jewelry. The men greet with something like, "Hi Butthead. You still driving that piece of crap?"

(Note: The forgoing are strictly the unscientific opinions expressed by our weekend revelers. Most are not documented by research. If you disagree with any of them, you're probably right. - JDH)

Words & Meaning

---

*Three Little Words * The Phone * Maxim Madness * In Context * Dogs Don't Talk * Opinion-Stated-As-Fact * Fighting * Names * Cruel and Unusual Sentencing * Swearing 101 * Perfect Message * Mystery Eyes * Fiction*

Three Little Words

The use of those powerful three little words has undoubtedly changed world history. I know it has significantly impacted mine.

In a perfect world, you would only whisper "I love you," to one great love your whole life through. But if you're single and over thirty, it's not likely to be that simple. One must expect a false start or two. Or more. Probably more.

There are two versions of the phrase. There's the one that means I'm crazy, head-over-heels, hopelessly, romantically in love with you. And there's a second, less potent version people use to remind loved ones that they are special.

There's also a third use of the three little words, actually more of a misuse, in which people use them to escape the consequences of boorish behavior or as a shortcut to being universally viewed as a loving person.

I once left a message with a woman whose answering machine message ended with "I love you." Think about it. She loves telemarketers, wrong numbers, her ex (who she just finished destroying in open court), burglars who are about to steal her blind, lawyers for the other side, the phone company, collection agencies, obscene phone callers, and everybody else indiscriminately. Do they feel "special" when she tells them she loves them? I don't think so.

My friend Orme told me his ex-girlfriend regularly berated him for his (imagined, he assures me) shortcomings, then would smile and say, "You know I love you." He said he didn't feel loved, but found it difficult to be angry with someone who just said she loved him. I think we call that manipulation. She gives him a shot, then escapes the consequences.

It's the version #1 three little words that intrigues me most. I don't suppose the census questionnaire asked how many people have said it how many times to how many other people. So I'll have to guess.

I'd say on average, during his or her lifetime, each person tells four people he or she is in love with them.

The first time is during the teen raging hormones period when one is too young to know any better and the romance ultimately breaks up because one or the other goes off to school or meets someone who owns a car.

A second time is for a failed, bittersweet romance that one mistakenly thought was going somewhere.

The third time one says "I love you" and follows up with marriage.

And, assuming that union ends, a fourth time after that when romance rekindles.

Okay, make it five. You should have a throw-away "I love you" to use foolishly, in a moment of unreality or deep passion; a moment you regret almost immediately.

I sometimes think about all the times I almost said it but

didn't. For instance, once my dancing partner and I were really grooving to Michael Jackson's "Beat It." When it was over, we laughed, hugged, and she said, "Oh I love you."

So I just gave her an extra squeeze and kissed her lightly on the neck.

Going directly from "Beat It" to an "I love you" declaration was more transition than I could handle. I'd needed time to think. And "I like you a lot, too," seemed a bit weak. Maybe she meant it as a version #2

She's married now but, so powerful are those words, that they still resonate in my memory nearly a decade later even though I don't remember anything else we said to each other.

According to some experts, one utterance of "I love you" is a sort of a freebie and doesn't fit any of the scenarios described above.

I heard a noted therapist tell her audience that anything one said during sex was okay, and not something they had to honor later. Her point was that passionate intimacy was a sort of temporary insanity. And that no prudent person should ever take the word of anyone so obviously whacko.

It's was probably such a moment that inspired the Fred Astair/Jane Powell song in the movie "Royal Wedding." Its title: "How Could You Believe Me When I Said I Loved You When You Know I've Been A Liar All My Life?"

The Phone

I seldom call women because I'm uncomfortable talking on the phone.

I'm not sure why. It has something to do with not being able to see the person I'm talking to ...And not being able to gage her interest in what I'm saying. I can't tell whether she's smiling or frowning or looking bored or baring her teeth. It's like talking to someone who's wearing those mirrored sunglasses. Or a bag over her head.

Also, I don't know how to end a conversation. I once had a male friend who was the same way. We avoided calling each other because neither of us knew how to end the darn thing. We talked far beyond anything we had to say. There were long pauses and a whole lot of drivel. We'd both squirm in our chairs as time passed. I guess he was squirming. I couldn't see him, so how do I know? His voice had a squirm sound to it. That's the thing I don't like about phone conversations. They're all audio and no video.

I envy people who have long telephone conversations. A woman friend was telling me about the guy she met and how nice he is. He calls her every night. By contrast, I get to hear this sort of thing a lot: "We had such a good time (on our last date) then you never called again." Well, I'd quarrel with the word "never" because I still might call. It could happen. But she's right. I don't call. Maybe I should just stop by.

Nah.

I don't much care for the way most other people end phone conversations either. Ending a phone conversation graciously, convincingly and without bruising the other person's fragile ego is an art few people master. There's a lot of bad phone etiquette going on out there.

I think my most unfavorite is someone who calls, delivers a prolonged soliloquy, then announces, "Gotta go." And hangs up.

"What just happened there?" I ask myself. Was it really necessary for me to stop what I was doing and hold the phone to my ear for all that time? When I was a newspaper reporter, one such woman called the city room and rambled on, uninterruptible, about her trivia. So the answering reporter put the phone down and continued his work, picking it up at intervals to say, "Yep" or "Uh-huh." When we realized what he was doing, each of us in turn picked up the phone, said "Yes ma'am" or "Right," until after a time someone noticed that the line was dead. Apparently she had to go. In the real world, with real friends, it's important to validate them, to show an interest in the conversation and to imply reluctance to end it.

"Can we continue this later? I'm snowed under just now."

"I've got company. Can I call you back?"

I had a friend who ended conversations with short words spoken very fast. "Okay," she'd say quickly and a bit clipped. "Yep. Okay then." It always ended the conversation but it was disconcerting — like trying to have a conversation with someone on the "up" escalator when you're on the "down."

It also works to sound reluctant to end the conversation, but bound by duty. "Well, if I'm going to have twelve dinner guests in an hour, I suppose I ought to start preparing something to feed them."

Or, my favorite for pure creativity:

(As an aside:) "That's a bazooka, dear. No I don't know if it's loaded. Put it back in Daddy's display case." (Into the phone:) "Can you excuse me for a moment? I have to take care of something."

Maxim Madness

There are so many rules, maxims, aphorisms, rationales, and cop-outs bandied about on the subject of dating, they can't all be valid. In fact, sometimes I think few are.

Here's my take on, variously, a rule, a syndrome, a communication, a game, a rationale, a cop-out and a fiction. Feel free to disagree.

1. *The Third Date Rule* holds that on the third date a couple has sex. There is, of course, no such rule. Think about it. Who would write such a rule? And where? And finally, who would be dumb enough to actually follow it? (The rule, of course, is valid on Cimemax late night movies where they seem to have a first and second date rule also.)

2. *E-mail Communication.* If your phone rings, you answer it. If you get a phone message, written or recorded, you return it forthwith. So why do you take six days to answer your e-mail? Is it because you don't get a blinking red light or an annoying beep like you do from your answering machine? Answer it anyway. It may jump-start your social life.

3. *Dating As a Game.* Dating should be fun, but not a

game. Most two-person games have one winner and one loser. Dating, especially the first date, should rise above that. I have a friend who said she took much of the angst out of dating by thinking of it as an audition. Sometimes she gets the part and sometimes she turns it down. But, whichever it is, she knows why she's on the date. It's not some inane game played by ill-defined rules. It's show biz.

4. *The Still Water Runs Deep Rationale.* It doesn't always. Sometimes that strong, silent date is silent because he/she is dull, unimaginative and can't think of anything to say. Sometimes, just sometimes, still water is not a deep lake but a puddle.

5. *The Conventional Wisdom Cop Out.* If you say it's conventional wisdom, you don't have to prove it, document it, or take responsibility for it. You credit it to some shadowy "they" — probably the same "they" who made up rule #1 above.

6. *The Fighting Fiction* holds that fighting is a normal, healthy and constructive part of any relationship. Actually, discussion of differences is all those things, but fighting isn't. Fighting is destructive and childish. It leaves scars, fosters mistrust, and ends relationships.

7. *The "I'll Call You" Lie.* Women are right: Some men say those words, then don't follow up. And it's understandable — not excusable, perhaps — but understandable. Look at it this way:

Amid the rousing beat of pagan dance music; the disorienting flicker of hypnotic colors splashing randomly across a crowded dance floor; the inevitable, inexorable, relentless, pounding flow of hormones surging through his veins; the air dripping with the promise of romance and a better life; and his ever burgeoning self-confidence soaring toward Mars, he probably means those words. It could happen.

Then comes the next morning. The alarm clock. The commute. Work. Steady, harsh lights, street sounds, weather and the myriad responsibilities and preoccupations of the real world. And with them, second thoughts. Loss of ardor. Foot dragging. And less emboldened motives. A deadened sense of adventure. “Where did I put that phone number?”

Meanwhile by a silent phone across town sits a once-trusting woman — scorned, disappointed, and angry at the way men promise to call, then don’t. Perfidy.

In my view, women have the syndrome right, but the motive wrong. It has very little to do with them. Those men aren’t sleazy, they’re just a tad wimpy and confused. More to be pitied than scorned.

Well, okay, maybe a bit sleazy too.

In Context

The most angry I ever made my ex-girlfriend was when she called me aggressive and I thanked her for it.

I thought I wasn't aggressive and was supposed to be. That's what my wrestling coaches told me in school. Also every dateless Saturday night, my well-meaning buddies chided my lack of aggressiveness. Now I have my own business, and people say, "Be aggressive. Get on the phone and sell." But I'm not that kind of aggressive and the telephone is not my favorite arena.

If there's a lesson here, I think it is that listening is not enough. One must understand. There are two `aggressive' words — one I ought to be and one I ought not to be. And my old friend was using the latter as I should have known from the way she spat it out.

Aggressive is not the only such word. "Sensitive" and "independent" are two more.

The loudest, brassiest, most offensive man I know insults people for sport. Yet this latter-day Don Rickles describes himself as excessively sensitive. Incredible. Freddy Kruger is more sensitive than he is. It turns out he means he has tender feelings that are easily hurt, not that he is attuned to — or in any way concerned about — the feelings of others.

In a recent discussion, a woman told me that, unlike when she was married, she was now very independent. My stomach cramped. My experience has been that "independent" is a woman's code word meaning she is seeking vengeance on the world for all the years she spent obediently attending to her children's needs and her husband's demands. "No more Ms. nice guy." Now she's free to be obstinate, distant, uncooperative, non-supportive, headstrong, difficult and totally focused on her own needs to the exclusion of anyone else's. "My children are having a hard time adjusting to my new independence," she might typically observe. Indeed.

Not being a mind reader, this totally nice woman from the discussion was a bit surprised by my reaction. By independent, she explained, she meant self-sufficient, centered, focused, reliable, competent and at ease with herself. Those happen to be among the qualities I value most in a woman — and men and children.

I still don't fully understand my ex-girlfriend's definition of aggressive. I'd ask her, but I fear she's too independent to answer and I'm much too sensitive to hear it.

Dogs Don't Talk

When **I was a kid,** the most popular member of my family was our dog Pepper.

Everybody loved him. And that was in large part, I think, because he didn't talk. He couldn't. He was an animal. As a non-talker, he didn't complain, or argue, or talk-back. Unlike us humans, he was never sarcastic, or insulting, or moody, or self-involved, or boring. He didn't lie, or exaggerate, or monopolize the telephone. And that, I believe, explains his charm and that of most domestic animals.

Yet, when Sophie calls her boyfriend Orme an animal, it's not intended as a compliment. By "animal," she probably means a totally unrefined person; an uncouth, self-involved, thoughtless slob who leaves his dirty laundry strewn across the floor of his train-wreck of an apartment.

But if you're a woman and your boyfriend calls you an animal, it may be high praise — especially during love making. It can mean sexy, uninhibited, energetic; a full, imaginative, enthusiastic participant in intimacies. A woman who runs with the wolves, so to speak.

Is that a double standard or what? I know it's unfair, but I'm not sure to which gender.

To be painfully precise about it, we are animals — as opposed to minerals and vegetables. We're not fish, fowl or reptiles either. We're animals.

As a youngster, I always thought we were much like other animals except that we were smarter. Some of us. That excuses a lot of crass behavior. And a lot of irresistible, primal, animal urges passed along through eons of time from our animal ancestors. Chalked it all up to evolution. See? It's not our fault.

Animals (the other ones) can't talk because they don't have voice boxes or the necessary ability to control their breathing. I read that in a book written by my brother Bert. And most of them don't have lips in the sense that we do. I'm glad I didn't find that out until after I'd read Doctor Doolittle to my kids. Try to picture your pet dog — or any dog — puckering up his lips to say the word "wow" or giving you an affectionate peck on the cheek.

When we were kids, Bert, two years my elder, told me that the principal difference between us and the animals was that we have opposable thumbs and were therefore able to use tools and build civilizations.

I thought we were smarter too, but didn't mention it to Bert. Perhaps we got smart while building civilizations using our opposable thumbs. Certainly Bert would have mentioned it if we'd been smarter at the outset.

Now, all these years later, I've learned from Bert's book that animals don't have selective memory either. That is, they can't sit down with a cup of coffee, put their feet up, and reminisce about their carefree youths, agonize over past mistakes, or plan for the future. They live pretty much in the present — which may be psychologically healthy but would severely limit conversation. No one wants to talk with a furry little thing that can neither reminisce, reason nor predict. Happily, we can do all three.

People routinely talk to their pets without expecting a reply. We, on the other hand, are expected to respond even when a passing stranger casually wishes us a good morning.

Most therapists recommend talking and listening as a means of jump-starting troubled relationships. They contend that one can be every bit as charming as one's dog while continuing to talk. The trick, it seems, is to stop saying the things that annoy people.

I agree. I think talking also performs a very profound and essential function in man-woman relationships: Only by talking can couples hope to undo the damage done by the talking they did previously.

Opinion-Stated-As-Fact

I **was very proud of** my practice of never talking about myself when I spoke before fellow students in the Dale Carnegie Course some years ago. It seemed to me virtuously modest. And, as an ex-newspaper reporter, it gave my contributions (in my then-opinion) an air of objectivity. Several of the instructors suggested I speak, instead, from experience, but I persisted. What did they know?

Years later, a facilitator at a discussion meeting took me to task for my pronouncements on the differences between men and women in their approaches to life. Being a man, I presumed to describe how men feel. "Speak from you own experience," she said. "That is my own experience," I replied with some indignation. But it wasn't. It was my own opinion-stated-as-fact. And there's a world's difference between the two.

At the recent retreat weekend, we had an open discussion in one of the cabins - complete with facilitator. Because of the informal surroundings, I suppose, no mention was made of speaking from the "I" position. It was kind of fun sitting there freely (if somewhat irresponsibly) tossing out opinions disguised as fact. I enjoyed it. It was a breach of most discussion guidelines. But it was fun for a change. I felt much the free agent and even joined-in with a couple of pronouncements of my own.

The more articulate members of the group were telling everyone what it was like to be out of "your" marriage. How much anger was there. And always would be. They nodded in agreement and built on the scenario they had created. They told the group how long it takes to transition out and the steps "you" go through. "But the anger is always there," they said.

Then I noticed some people weren't talking at all. Did they agree? Were they believing what they were hearing? Did they think there was something wrong with them if they weren't angry? Were they dreading the anger that, according to the scenario, was sure to come? Perhaps they were reluctant to speak from personal experience when others didn't seem required to do likewise? Or did they just not want to make waves?

I still don't know the answers, of course. But the experience was useful. It demonstrated to me first-hand why speaking from experience works so well, and why opinion-stated-as-fact can sabatoge a potentially enlightening discussion.

Fighting

I **'ve always blanched** at the term "fighting fair," as if fighting is a given in relationships and there's some virtue in improving one's technique.

In the discussions I've attended, the consensus was that fighting is the Roto-Rooter of clogged communications; that couples who don't fight are suppressing some fierce hostility that will eventually shatter the relationship, leaving heartbreak, disillusion and estrangement in its wake. And that fighting somehow prevents such mayhem.

I've never understood that. Conflict is probably inevitable between human beings. And couples, after all, are made up of two unique people who grew up separately, had their own experiences, and were reared in different families. One lives life as a man, the other as a woman. How different can you get?

Reacting with a flash of anger when one's buttons are inadvertently pushed is understandable. But fighting? Nix.

Grown people who yell and try to invalidate each other are not really grown people at all. And what they create is not clarity, but unkind words that will hang in the air between them forever.

174. - Single Over Thirty

Fighting leaves scars.

I never heard my parents fight. I never heard my brothers fight with their wives (although when we were kids, we fought with each other all the time — so I know they know how.) I never fought with my ex-wife. And while we were married, people said that was the reason our marriage lasted. When we finally were divorced, they said lack of fighting was the reason it didn't last longer.

Not being a proponent of fighting, I'm probably the least qualified to explain just what the benefit is. I don't feel relaxed and relieved after a fight — not even a verbal one. I feel beat up.

Granted, I can think of a couple of times when someone in the heat of a fight has blurted out something useful. "You don't treat me as an adult," for instance. That would be valuable information for me. I want to treat all adults as adults. Most of the time, I even want to treat children as adults. But if I heard that message in the midst of a screaming match with a girl friend, my focus would be on defending myself from her anger and accusations.

If I could put words together at all while my adrenaline was pumping that hard, I'd probably say something destructive like, "Try acting like an adult if you want to be treated like one."

If she said the same thing to me while we were having a calm, unthreatening discussion, I would hear her. I would ask caring questions. I would try to catch myself in the infraction and correct it.

Perhaps it's time to define terms. Maybe what I call a discussion of differences, is what the consensus calls fighting. And what I call fighting, they call World War III.

So here, by my definition, are 13 symptoms of fighting in a relationship:

1. The decibel level rises.
2. If one has ever been his or her partner's advocate, he or she stops for the duration of the fight.
3. Either partner feels escalating anger during the interaction.
4. Either partner feels free to bring into the discussion old grievances.
5. The use of profanity expands.
6. The object of the exercise becomes winning instead of solving problems.
7. The participants cease to treat each other with respect.
8. They try to hurt each other and place blame on the other.
9. Either participant touches the other in a non-loving way.
10. Either partner refuses to be touched in a loving way by the other.
11. Either partner attributes unworthy motives to the other.
12. Either partner leaves the fight in anger, frustration or fear.
13. Either partner threatens to call off the relationship or take other retaliatory action.

I'm not suggesting that "Fighting Fair" should not be discussed. I just think it should be discussed as part of another topic; "Relationship Myths," for instance.

Names

If you get a message on your answering machine from "Miss," "Ms.," "Mr.," or "Mrs." anybody, you can be fairly sure you don't know them and that they're from local government, the phone company or a collection agency. Those people don't have first names. The rest of the world, however, identifies itself more fully.

You can tell a lot about people by how they use their names.

When you call a place of business and the voice that answers says "Ajax Company, this is Sally," it's safe to assume that Sally is either a temp or a go-fer. Movers and shakers use their full names. All except the boss. The more imposing he is, the shorter his name gets. The president, chairman, chief executive officer, founder and principal stock holder of a major corporation, for instance, is likely to sign his name with something disarming like "Bud." He doesn't answer phones that way, of course, because he doesn't answer phones..

It wasn't always that way. But times have changed. Formality is out, chumminess is in. Everyone who is any-one in the work-a-day world signs his or her first name only (under which may be printed his full, formal name and position). First names also work well on answering machines and in social and recreational settings.

Of course doctors, dentists, clergy, congressmen and presidents use titles. That seems a bit pretentious to me. Oh, perhaps it's okay for a president. But if a doctor calls me "John," as I prefer, I call him by his first name, which he seems not to prefer. But it seems only fair. Besides, I love to see the wince that follows and the way his nurses start whispering uneasily. Dentists are the same. My young dentist put a new engine in my VW when he was in college. Now he's a doctor of dental surgery who regularly jams my mouth with sterilized, stainless steel picks, clamps and drills — probably so I can't call him "Marty" in front of his staff. He manages not to use my name at all.

The pre-printed name tags used at special singles social events often have a big first name (that can be read from across the room) and a small last name (that requires close proximity and a certain amount of interest in the wearer.)

At the more informal discussion meetings, people make their own name tags. Most use both first and last names. But not me. You wouldn't believe how many discussions I've had during the break about my last name.

My father had a nice response to questions about his last name. He explained that in Biblical days everyone's name was Husband. And one-by-one, as they committed sins, their names were changed.

There are very few of us left.

Note: *Husband* is actually an English name meaning farmer (as in "animal husbandry") and having no relationship to marital status. (Or sins committed.)

Cruel and Unusual Sentencing

Don't look now, but the English language is changing at an alarming rate. It's not just the words. They've always changed to keep up with the times. It's the way words are delivered.

The three newly introduced modes are:

1. Uptalk
2. Right-pausers and
3. The Gumble Grumble

In "up-talking," the pitch of the last few words is raised so it sounds like a question even though it isn't. It's used mostly in a simple declaration as in "Godiva has these new chocolates with raisins in them." There's an implied uncertainty there, as if the speaker is not sure they're really raisins. Maybe they're currants, or lumpy chocolate or even candied ants.

Most up-talkers seem to be recent graduates which makes me think they are actually taught to up-talk. Besides, up-talking would work so well in the classroom. When one is called upon to recite, one may be wrong. But it doesn't seem so grievous an error in up-talk. It's as if the up-talker warned listeners that he might be wrong — simply in the process of using up-talk. Nobody can not like an up-talker. They're so human, so uncertain, so willing — even eager — to be wrong, so cuddly, unimposing and unthreatening.

Not so with "right-pausers". They involve you in their idle patter whether you like it or not. He or she (men seem to do it more than women) stops at the end of each sentence and says "right?" followed by dead air. You, the listener, are then required to validate his sentence before he continues on to the next. So you say "right". And he gives you another sentence followed by "right?" and more dead air.

It's not as if he were explaining that the pressure in a combustion chamber climbs to a psi equal to the square root of the downward thrust of the propellant quotient squared. (That's how rocket scientists talk. Probably.)

But no, the conversation in which the right-pauser has entrapped you is bland, stream-of-consciousness stuff that can make you feel like an idiot saying "okay" and "right" and "uh" at the end of each of his empty sentences.

There is a "Type A" variant of right-pausing, however, that isn't so bad. In it, the speaker, often a heavy coffee drinker, doesn't pause after saying "right?," but continues on without you. Bless him and every one of his frazzled little nerve endings.

There is also a new tense to the English language. It could be called the "Gumble Grumble" after the former Today Show's Bryan Gumble who is a one-tense man. The new tense simply describes the future as if it were the present. Like "We're out of here." (They're not out of here at all. They're still here. I can see them plain as day.) "But we're back on Monday." (Absurd. How can they be back when they never left?) "And a famous grammarian is here on

Tuesday to discuss speech aberrations." (And we all know what Topic No. 1 should be, don't we?)

Swearing 101

You know you shouldn't swear. But if you're going to do it anyway, damn it all, do it right.

Used properly, swearing can actually work for you. It can be disarming and suggest you are leveling with people and that you won't be shocked or fall apart under pressure. It can add a light touch in a tense situation.

If done well, swearing can be very chic — add to your charm and bon vivance. People will see it more as colorful language than actual swearing.

Dropping a swear word in a place where it does not belong as a means of humorous emphasis can be a delight — especially if all the other words are high-sounding and dignified.

It can also be used effectively for emphasis. But in all uses of profanity, you need to go by the rules. And here they are:

1. *Don't swear in writing.* Proper swearing is an aural phenomenon, designed to be heard, not seen. Words that were so funny at the cocktail party look atrocious scrawled on a wall or written in a report.

2. *Don't swear early in the day.* Good swearing is like good liquor. Late in the day or evening when people are beginning to relax, a well placed profanity can be a great pick-me-up.

3. *Don't swear on radio or TV or into a recording device.* At worst, recorded or broadcast swearing will be played back in the wrong context, to the wrong audience, and at the wrong time. At best, the radio and TV people will just hate you intensely for knocking them off the air.

4. *Don't swear in a string.* A long and varied string of swear words tied together in a single sentence is overkill and grosses people out.

5. *Don't let it become a habit.* You should always be in control of your own swearing. Profane words should never "just slip out."

6. *Don't use swear words that conjure up ugliness.* Originally, swear words were coined by low-lifes because of their shock value. They were either outrageously sacrilegious or they described anti-social objects, activities and body parts. However, heavy usage has diluted their meanings until people seldom think of a swear word's literal meaning when they utter it or hear it. Such words have taken on an imprecise meaning of their own. An innocuous example: The word damn no longer conjures up visions of the flames of Hades. Likewise, people don't think of the activity when one mentions the f word or the substance when one utters the s word. But one is likely to picture the activity or substance when one hears swear words that are rare enough to still be descriptive. Such words and combinations of words should never be used.

7. *Don't swear "at" people.* People will hate you if you say unkind things to them — swearing or not. Tax forms, foreign governments with whom we are at war, and people who take up two parking spaces at the supermarket, however, are rather obvious exceptions.

8. *Don't swear too often.* Timing is everything. I went to a meeting recently where the moderator good-naturedly used the f word. Men and women alike tittered with delight at his daring and candor. So he used it again and his audience decided he was a jerk.

9. *Never swear when you are angry.* Times haven't changed that much. Swearing an oath because you are angry is just as unseemly, uncivilized, unnerving, and out-of-control as it ever was. It puts adults off and scares little children. Don't do it.

10. *Choose your audience well.* First you should know your audience — whether one person or a group — well enough to predict what effect a well-placed swear-word will have. It's not wise to take a chance. And it's not appropriate to swear in front of your parents, children, strangers, some clergy and most clients. When in doubt, don't swear.

11. *Don't apologize for swearing.* That's what my country friends call "peeing in the soup". You create something dashing and creative, then you ruin it by apologizing.

12. *Don't swear pretentiously.* Don't swear as a means of getting on a buddy-buddy basis with someone you view as having great stature. Just because the boss swears in front of you is no reason you should swear to the same extent in front of him. Chances are you'll do it poorly and he'll see right through your patronizing pretense.

13. *Don't let TV censors be your guide.* True, television still refrains from heavy-duty cuss words, but prime-time TV does use substantial words and they swear in anger — and at people. That's okay for them. They're not real. You, on the other hand, are. So don't be surprised when your audience doesn't respond the same as NYPD Blue's.

One final note: If you aren't comfortable swearing, don't. These guidelines are intended primarily for people who are going to swear anyway. They are presented here under the premise that anything you are going to do anyway is worth doing well.

Perfect Message

In a recent Seinfeld re-run, dysfunctional George convinces himself that the way to his date's heart is to tell her he loves her. As they park in his car, he looks her straight in the eye and says the magic words, "I love you," to which she replies, "Let's get something to eat."

Terrible answer, perfect message.

The answer is not responsive. It's also rather rude, invalidating, self-involved, ignorant, shallow, insensitive, and if they follow her suggestion, it could even be fattening.

But there's no missing the message.

Clearly, the message is: "Get real, George, you're in this thing all by yourself."

I had a similar experience when an old friend popped up at a social weekend. All I said as we walked to the dance floor was "It's so nice to see you again. I've missed you." She said "A lot of new faces here this weekend."

Though I might have preferred her to say, "Not as much as I've missed you, Cowboy," her comment was nevertheless useful. I could see immediately we were not of a like mind. But we danced anyway and my stepping on her foot was an accident.

Mystery Eyes

I **have never personally met** an extraterrestrial, but I did meet a guy who claims he can tell everything about a woman by looking deeply into her eyes.

Just as I was about to ask him for a ride in his space ship, he explained he was fed up with all the talk these days about Internet romances, Myers-Briggs scores, compatibility tests, non-negotiables, and the like. He said he can tell by looking into a pretty woman's eyes whether she is honest, loyal, loving, a good match for him, and a whole lot more. "The eyes tell it all," he said. "All you really have to do is look — really look."

In my view, staring deeply into someone's eyes is more likely to freak them out — sort of like sticking your finger in their ear. You had better know them very well. And even then, all you'll see is two eyes looking back at you. Granted, sometimes they're such lovely eyes, clear, colorful and twinkly, that one is transported. But there's no real information there.

There is, of course, information about mood and temperament in the area surrounding the eye. The angle of eyebrows, the droop of eyelids, a squint, a wink, or tears can speak volumes. But the eyes themselves are mute.

188. - Single Over Thirty

To make my quest for eye statements more authentic, I performed some first-hand research. I stared into a pretty woman's eyes. I stood back far enough to get her eyes in focus. Still, all I saw was eyelids, eyelashes, two retinas, two iris, two cornea and my own reflection. Twice. No privileged information. No tell-tale character traits. No secret agendas. Perhaps I didn't look long enough or deeply enough. I'd have lingered there longer but my test subject said the experiment was annoying and asked me to stop. So much for the scientific approach.

I came away more convinced than ever that eyes are like those one-way mirrors police use to secretly watch suspects in the interrogation room. If you're standing on the right side of them, you can see a great deal. If not, you see only yourself. If it's information you seek, eyes are clearly for looking out of, not into.

I'm currently re-reading an old James Bond novel in which Bond remarks that arch villain Blofeld's "dark green, glass eyes were unfathomable." Of course they were. Bond was looking through them backwards.

Remember the adage "Eyes are the windows of the soul"? Well, forget it. According to Bartlett's Book of Familiar Quotations, there is no such quote. It's probably a distortion of William Blake's 1818 verse:

This life's dim windows of the soul
Distorts the Heavens from pole to pole
And leads you to believe a lie
When you see with, not through, the eye

I have no idea what that means.

Fiction

Mrs. Morgan, who ran the Mom and Pop grocery store of my youth, told me she listened to radio soap operas "to learn about life." I was impressed and went home to recommend that my mother follow her example — to which my mother wisely replied, "ppffft." And she was right.

As time went on and I experienced real life, I began to realize just how wrong Mrs. Morgan was. Radio and TV soap operas are about how life isn't. So are movies, dramas, situation comedies and most talk shows. What entertains us most is anything that is screwball, bizarre or dysfunctional. And the more-so, the better.

Lovable, goofy Lucy screws up everything and Ricky thinks that's just wonderful. I dated a woman once who told me she grew up with no father and no siblings. She watched TV much of the time while her mother worked. With no other frame of reference, "I Love Lucy" became her standard for loving relationships. She saw herself as Lucy. And what disappointed her most about her boyfriends was that their responses fell short of Ricky's.

Another woman told me she and her ex-husband were like Ozzie and Harriet Nelson, but there was nothing in the long-run TV comedy to prepare her for her Ozzie running off with his 24-year-old secretary.

In real life, if you go out on a date and argue all evening, that's a pretty sure sign that you and your date are not compatible. In the movies, it's a sign that opposites attract; that fate will intercede; that you'll marry and, inexplicably, live in peace and harmony ever after.

One of my favorite all-time TV shows is "Seinfeld," a situation comedy about four (or five if you count Newman) of the most dysfunctional people imaginable. And it's hilarious. But as much as I love the show, I wouldn't come within ten feet of those guys in real life.

Still, all that is kind of funny, absurd and relatively harmless. The real danger comes when people identify with the bad guys in dramas. Or when the good guys, like Rambo and Dirty Harry, leave such a trail of corpses in their wakes that it sends a distorted message about the value of human life.

In TV dramas, "cool" high school kids take drugs and join gangs. And it's chic for clean-cut young people to have indiscriminate, unprotected sex. Often. On the hit show, "Friends," Rachel is upset so she brings home some sleazy guy she just met and sleeps with him. Later, on a whim, she gets a tattoo. Not even Lucy would have done that. Rachel and her friends are sooo cool, it must be tempting for their real-life peers to think of the TV show's make-believe antics as normal and their own lives as overly cautious and out-of sync with what's really happening.

Sometimes I think movies, TV shows, sitcoms, plays and the like should have warnings like packs of cigarettes: "Danger. This show is nonsense and should not be confused with real life. People don't really act this way. They don't get this much sex. They don't wreck cars, blow up buildings or kill people — not even bad guys — and if they did, they'd at least feel bad about it. Do not attempt to imitate what you see on this show at the risk of going to prison, contracting a social disease, becoming a single parent, and losing your friends, your job, your health and your safe-driver insurance discount.

Ethics & Character Issues

*Lies * The Autonomous Truth * Privilege * She's Independent * Trait or Habit * Standards * With All Their Faults*

Lies

How can you disdain all liars when sometimes people lie for virtuous reasons? Besides, everybody lies. And anyone who says he or she doesn't is playing fast and loose with the truth.

Scott Peck, author of The Road Less Traveled, says it isn't the lie, but the motive behind it that should be judged. And I agree. In fact, I'd go one step further and say we ought to have different names for different kinds of lies. Calling them all lies levels the playing field, tainting virtuous liars, while boosting the standing of malicious liars. Here's my list beginning with the least egregious:

Honest mistake — An untruth spoken out of misunderstanding or misinformation.

Story — An untruth told to protect or enhance the innocence of children or to allay their fears.

Graciousness — An untruth designed to protect the sensibilities or well-being of others.

Brevity edit — A bending of the truth purely in the interest of keeping conversation moving.

Jolly — An imaginative, fictional untruth told for entertainment purposes only, usually voluntarily corrected by the teller at a later time.

Cover story — An untruth told under pressure to protect one's own physical well being.

Half-truth — The omission of certain salient facts from an otherwise truthful account to create a self-serving mis-impression.

Sloth — An untruth spoken out of laziness or lack of respect for the truth or out of general, habitual inexactness.

Stonewall — A steadfast untruth told out of vanity, intransigence or self-aggrandizement by people who are afraid to admit they're wrong, very often compounding an earlier untruth.

Hot breath — An untruth told as a means of controlling or manipulating others.

Lie — A malicious untruth told to escape work, punishment or responsibility. Or to inflict pain and suffering on others.

Obscenity — A perfidious untruth told for personal gain by someone in a position of public, religious or professional trust.

Here's a self-test: One of the Los Angeles law enforcement higher-ups maintained that O.J. Simpson was not a suspect when four detectives arrived without a warrant at Simpson's home — ostensibly to notify him of the murders. The official told the court that sending four detectives was not uncommon, but when pressed, could not recall the department ever having done it before.

Assuming, as the jury apparently did, that he was not

speaking the truth, which of the above would you say he was speaking?

The Autonomous Truth

"**Your truth may not be** my truth. Everybody has their own truth," a lawyer friend told me when I insisted that discovering the truth was important to me.

I thought about that for a moment — which seemed like plenty of time — then I agreed. After all, when half a dozen people witness the same event, don't they all give slightly different versions of it? And don't they all swear their version is the truth?

Still, something about that rationale bothered me. There really is a truth, you know — a truth that has nothing to do with memories, or opinions, or theories, or self-interest, or you, or me. It's the genuine article, unfettered by interpretations. Granted, often it goes undiscovered, but it's there nevertheless. It's the autonomous truth and nobody owns it.

Discovering the truth as I'm using the term has little to do with ethics. It's about getting life to work more smoothly. The truth is a key. No matter who uses the it, it works. If everyone you know, including your clergy, your sainted mother, and the great love of your life, all said you should use "copy" instead of "install" to load your new software, it still wouldn't work. Unless it were true, of course. Then it would work no matter who said it.

The kind of non-truth that seems to get the most attention these days is lying. But I don't worry a whole lot about that. Lies and liars are relatively easy to track. And as a rule they get all tangled up in their own words.

The most destructive kind of non-truth for me is the kind I feed myself. I call that the convenient truth; the path of least resistance. It takes the place of knowing the real answer. It makes it unnecessary to say "I don't know" when one doesn't know. It makes one an authority without having to compile real knowledge. It makes things seem to fit that don't. Sometimes it's a statement, sometimes an attitude. And because it's one's very own, it can be inordinately difficult to recognize.

Let's say in high school I got poor grades in Spanish (which I did.) A year later I took French and it was a disaster. So rather than recognize that learning languages is hard work that requires doing one's homework, I decide I have no talent for languages. My truth. Cool move. No more suffering through languages classes for this teenager.

The convenient truth (as distinguished from the autonomous truth) includes accepting false premises, making assumptions, employing flawed formulas, investing foolish trust in unworthy people and institutions, locking onto old prejudices, rushing to judgement, accepting willy-nilly so-called conventional wisdom, believing old wives tales, and mindlessly going along with the crowd.

As I was riding upwards in the glass elevator in my office building, I spotted a friend far below. When I told her about it later, she said, "Boy you don't miss much, do you?"

I agreed, thereby including "I don't miss much" as part of

my truth. Insightful woman, I thought. But the real truth is I have no idea how much I miss because I miss it.

Privilege

I am a man of privilege.

Late in the evening after a family reunion in Charleston, West Virginia, my brother and I were stopped by a disheveled black woman who asked us for money. I gave her some. When we caught up with the rest of the family at the hotel, they were shocked and dismayed. "She got money off you?" one of my small-town in-laws said.

"No," I said. "I *gave* her money. There's a difference."

I get enough to eat — every day. I sleep in warmth and safety. My teeth don't ache. I have no ominous, untreated medical problems. I don't obsess over the welfare of my progeny. I have a job, a bank account, some possessions, a modicum of self esteem, and I feel good. That makes me a man of privilege in contrast to the lady who asked for money.

It wasn't always quite that good.

Some years ago, I was stopped outside the Bethesda Metro by a well-dressed man from the Middle East who was accompanied by his pre-teen daughter — also nicely dressed. Thinking he was asking for directions, I read the sheet he handed me and found he had lost his job and couldn't meet his bills. I shook my head "no" and moved on. "Oh Please." he called after me and started to cry. The experience bothered me for days. I had lost my job too.

On the half-block between my office in downtown Washington and the Metro, five or six street people wait in ambush every night at quitting time. I don't give money to them because it would be like giving out silver dollars on Halloween night. There'd be a line clear around the block waiting for me when I left work.

The woman I was with said she never gives money to "those people."

"I work hard for my money," she said. And she does. She has a well-paying government job, she owns a rather nice split level home, she is college educated, she grew up in relative comfort, she dresses stylishly, takes care of herself, and she's a knock-out. If that isn't privilege, I don't know what is. I was a shade disappointed by her lack of compassion.

Some of what she has, she provided for herself. But a good deal of it came from being born into a privileged life "those people" didn't enjoy. She was born in the United States to parents who loved her, gave her a comfortable childhood, and sent her to college. She's mentally stable and without physical handicaps. She deserves credit for working hard and taking care of herself, but being a knock-out is pure, unmitigated good luck. Even loving parents can't guarantee that.

If one ever gives to any charity, giving to street people seems like the best because it's the simplest. There are no administrative expenses involved. Unlike the American Red Cross, which mis-allocated much of the $988 million it raised for 9/11 victims, the end recipient gets it all. There are no "experts" in the middle deciding how to really spend your donation. You see exactly who gets it. It's immediate.

The look of genuine delight from the recipients is worth the price. And if you stick around, you may even see the recipient walk into a McDonalds and order up a Big Mac.

She's Independent

When this perfectly nice woman told me she was independent, I immediately got stomach cramps.

Then she told me she installed new kitchen cabinets by herself by devising a system of props and levers to keep the cabinets up there while she fastened them permanently to the wall. She went on to talk about the responsibilities of her job and how she works-out at the company gym after work.

She mentioned in passing that she volunteered to teach therapeutic horseback riding to disabled people and said she maintains a growing edge by taking courses on such diverse topics as construction techniques, accounting and photography. She has a cadre of friends for mutual support, going on long bike rides with one group, and getting together for monthly dinners with another.

My stomach cramps went away. She really is independent. And that's a good thing.

Usually when women say they are independent, I translate the term as "difficult."

Katrina was that way. After years of accommodating her

demanding husband, catering to her three children's every need, and being a general sweetheart to nearly everyone, her husband divorced her. So she took a long, hard look at her life and decided she had been a doormat. What she needed was to be more independent.

Now she makes a point of not automatically accommodating anyone. It's a good thing her children are now grown because she responds to them at her convenience, not theirs. She routinely disagrees with anyone foolish enough to express an opinion in her presence. After all, it's her right to disagree. She's independent.

I came upon her once at a weekend retreat trying to set a fire in the fireplace with just newspapers and logs. "Do you want me to get some kindling?" I asked.

"No, I don't need kindling," she said.

"You can't start a fire with just newspapers and big heavy logs," I said.

"Don't tell me what I can or cannot do," she said.

In a sense, of course, she was right. She actually did start the fire without kindling. In fact she started it about 20 times in succession until she ran out of paper.

That's what I call being difficult. But it's what Katrina calls being independent. In her book, she's making her own decisions and it feels good. She's independent.

I think I like the term self-reliant better. Someone who figures a way to install her own cabinets without help is certainly self-reliant. One who insists upon setting logs on fire with just a match and a back issue of The Washington Post probably isn't.

I like Katrina, although I may have liked the old Katrina a

bit better than the new one. In her marriage, her husband was always right and she accommodated him until she was blue in the face. Her reward for all that accommodation is that she gets to be single, middle-aged and alone.

Her remedy: Be independent -- with a vengeance.

My take on it is that she shouldn't have made any basic changes in her approach to people, although as a single person, she'd now have to take the full brunt of decision-making, chores, social life, finances, home repairs, car maintenance, furniture moving, jar opening and more. That, in my view, is the stuff real independence is made of.

Do men have a similar problem with toxic independence resulting from a failed marriage? You may disagree with me, but I think it's rare. If a single man is that difficult, chances are he's always been -- including during the marriage. He didn't react to his failed marriage by becoming independent; his marriage reacted to him by failing.

Trait or Habit?

There's a widely held belief that one should not commit to a love interest with the idea of changing him or her. And by extension, real love completely accepts people just as they are — no more, no less. The secret to lasting love, say the experts, is to accept your love interest "as is."

I agree with that. Most of the time. At least until the love interest in question belches at a formal dinner party and thinks it's cute.

Does one end a relationship over a belch? I don't think so. A belch is not a personality trait. It's a habit. You can change it. In fact, please change it.

Habits can be changed without changing the essential person. You've probably been modifying your habits for years, trading in the habits that don't work for those that do. That process is called "growth."

Traits, on the other hand, are what makes the person, the person. They can be admirable or despicable and acceptable or non-acceptable. But what they can't be is changed — not without some pretty extreme and dangerous procedures that probably won't work anyway. (i.e. hypnosis, psychoanalysis, electric shock treatment, mind altering drugs, support therapy and, if you want to be sure, a lobotomy.)

Recognizing one's own traits can be difficult because, to the bearer, they don't seem like traits. They're just you doing what comes naturally. You probably can't see them without help. They're like your face. Others see it directly and recognize you by it. You need a mirror or a photograph.

When someone else points out one of your traits, you may be surprised as I was when I agreed to leave my car, unlocked, in front of my house so the repair people could replace the windshield. I took a bus to work.

My daughter Margaret answered the phone when the repair foreman called later to say he was short-handed and needed to re-schedule. "I know my dad," she told him. "He won't reschedule, he'll cancel."

Right on. I was delighted on several counts: My windshield got replaced (the foreman did it himself), no more bus rides, and my daughter asserted herself intelligently. But most of all I was proud that she knew me by trait, not just by habit. (I'm not defending my intransigence, just reveling in Margaret's recognition of it.)

It's so important to recognize the difference between a habit and a trait. Without that critical recognition, one might foolishly dump a potential partner over a changeable bad habit (like belching or smoking,) while accepting one with an unchangeable flawed trait (like disloyalty, dishonesty or irresponsibility.)

And now for a little test. There are just three answers to the following 20 questions: Habit, trait and neither. The key to the correct answers is being able to tell which activities can be changed without a basic change of personality.

1. Watches the news at 11, then goes to bed.
2. Watches football on Sunday afternoons.
3. Won't answer the phone while watching football.
4. Prefers fiction over non-fiction books.
5. Keeps car, desk and dresser drawers neat and orderly.
6. Drinks heavily.
7. Snores.
8. Picks his nose.
9. Swears a blue streak.
10. Maligns the opposite sex.
11. Talks incessantly.
12. Smiles all the time.
13. Seldom smiles.
14. Loves fly fishing.
15. Has a mercurial temper.
16. Smokes.
17. Likes good music.
18. Listens to music all day long.
19. Likes cats.
20. Is allergic to cats.

Answers: 1-h, 2-h, 3-h, 4-t, 5-t, 6-n, 7-n, 8-h, 9-h, 10-t, 11-t, 12-t,13-t, 14-t, 15-t, 16-h, 17-t, 18-h, 19-t, 20-n. (Nos. 6, 7 and 20 are physical problems over which one may have no control.)

And, by the way, although the belching in paragraph two above is just a habit, thinking it's cute may very well be a trait. So be careful.

Standards

Most people would probably agree that a potential partner ought to share one's standards of behavior.

I certainly agree, although I'm not sure I know exactly what people mean by standards? Why do so many single people complain that they have trouble meeting prospects whose standards come up to theirs? I've never heard anyone grouse about the other's standards being too high; just too low. Actually, I've never heard anyone recognize higher standards than their own exist anywhere on the planet.

We joked about that phenomenon during a recent discussion on standards. One guy said he was so glad to be meeting with the people with high standards and not the alcoholic, infantile, unenlightened, scheming, unfaithful, nitpicking, insensitive, invalidating brutes they broke up with.

On the way home after the meeting, I couldn't help wondering what exactly one with low standards might be like. Certainly they would lie, cheat and steal. They would be deadbeats who do not clean themselves, their clothes or their teeth regularly.

Or would that be too obvious? A potential partner whose

standards didn't come up to one's own would need more subtle shortcomings -- otherwise associating with them might reflect poorly on one's own standards. They might brush their teeth, for instance, but not as often. They don't need to lie much, but they should lie more than their high-standard partner does. Typically, they might park in handicapped zones, turn off the ignition and lock the car, instead of parking in a fire zone and just running in to the store for a minute like those of us with high standards might do.

I brush twice a day. I suppose if I dated someone who brushes twice a day and carries a toothbrush in her purse so she can brush every time she has food, I might grudgingly have to admit she has higher standards than I do. I might also think she is a bit compulsive.

I would like just once to hear someone say (with a straight face) that they broke up because the other person's standards were too high.

By the time I put the car in the garage that evening, I had visualized what an interview with someone with low standards might be like -- someone like Suzybell's ex-boyfriend, Fritz, who runs a used auto parts shop on the edge of town:

Me: Suzybelle says she broke up with you because you have low standards. Do you have low standards?"

Fritz: "Yeah. That's right."

Me: "Why?"

Fritz: "It's how I was brought up. My whole family has low standards. I only hire people for the shop who have low standards."

Me: "Are you saying you prefer low standards?"

<u>Fritz:</u> "Yeah."

<u>Me:</u> "Why?"

<u>Fritz:</u> "It's easier. Fewer restrictions. You can do whatever you want; make more money with less effort. Gives you greater freedom and it isn't anal like high standards. You're never bothered by guilt or conscience."

<u>Me:</u> But it cost you your girlfriend."

<u>Fritz:</u> "Yeah. Poor Suzybelle. She was so up-tight. I had to break it off with her. Her standards just didn't come down to mine."

<u>Me:</u> "Oh come on. You're a business man. You have a reputation in the community to protect. Being known as a man with low standards must hurt business."

<u>Fritz:</u> "Nah, people only care about price. And I have the lowest prices in town. I'll show you what I mean. Is that your car parked out front?"

<u>Me:</u> "Yes."

<u>Fritz:</u> "What would you expect to pay to replace four hub caps?"

<u>Me:</u> "How would I know? I don't know the price of hub caps. And I don't need 'em. I've already got four."

<u>Fritz:</u> "No you don't."

With All Their Faults

The people at a discussion meeting on "opposite sex friends" had a much more stringent definition of friends than I do.

For me, it's all really rather simple. If I like them, they're a friend. If I like them and they are female, they become opposite sex friends. Sometimes people I wouldn't normally like but who seem to like me also become friends. Nobody but me decides who my friends are. And I don't even know why I choose them. I guess they're easy to be around. It doesn't get much more complicated than that. They need no special talents or character traits.

This view came clear to me when one guy at the meeting told of all the friends he thought he had until he had a crisis and needed their support. "I thought they were my friends, but when I needed them, they weren't there for me," he lamented.

I understand his disappointment, but I have a point of view of my own I would like to try on you. My experience has been that, friends or not, very few people are able to give real support when it's needed.

And requiring friends to call, ask you how you feel, offer to loan you their cars, listen to your woes at 3 a.m., drive you around, walk your dog, loan you money, help get you a job, or buy you ice cream is like requiring them to play Chopin's Polonaise in B Flat. They'd be glad to. It's just that they don't know how.

It could be they lack the skills. Or they may have been raised to think other people's crises are private and they would be intruding. They could be afraid they might cry if they get too close to friends' tragedies. They (the men) may not think it's masculine. They may lack the emotional energy. They may be involved in a personal crisis of their own which, though not as public as yours, is all they can handle. They could be afraid of emotional encounters, or be too shy to respond.

At the break a woman told me of a friend at work who, when she was in a spot, once drove her 12 miles out of his way.

"Was he a particularly close friend," I asked.

"Oh no, he's always doing things like that for people," she said.

In my view, he's a great guy, but not necessarily a friend — even after the 12-mile trip. A friend is not a friend because of how he or she responds in need. With all their faults, a friend is a friend because you chose them, you got to know them well, and you like them. And if in a crisis, they come through for you, that's the icing on the cake.

If not, dial 911.

The Only Constant is Change

*Ten Years Younger * Internet Romance * Women on the Beach * Women Asking for a Date * Happy Birthday*

Ten Years Younger

I **have a theory that**, beyond a certain age, all adults think they look ten years younger than they actually do. In their minds' eye, for instance, fifty-year-olds see themselves as forty-year-olds. And forty-year-olds as thirty.

There are several reasons for this.

Reason #1 — One doesn't see one's self on a daily basis as other people do, so subtle changes go largely unnoticed. Sure, you get an occasional glance in the mirror or a close-up view while shaving (men) or applying make-up (women.) But it takes those brief vignettes years to really register — ten years to be exact. Snap shots don't count because they're taken from too far away and, besides, everyone takes a lousy picture — just ask `em.

Reason #2 — The present always seems to get here a bit before we're ready to give up the past. I know it's true with me. If you question this, go ask your kids how old they are. I can almost guarantee that the same mind-set that keeps the parent (you) looking young refuses to let the kids grow up.

Reason #3 — We aren't really motivated to keep our mental visions of ourselves up to date. There's simply no payoff. It's bad enough that you have to keep your weight down, your waist slim, your car tuned, your bills paid, and your gutters clean. There's no good reason you also have to keep tabs on your personal aging process.

Reason #4 — It's Natures way. There's a reason evolution has positioned our eyes in such a way that we can see others but not ourselves. If there were any species among our evolutionary ancestors who could see themselves, they obviously did not survive. Small wonder. There are some things you're just better off not having to look at.

My daughter and I were looking through some photos recently when we came upon a picture of me. I told her it was taken during an excursion a few months ago. "No, Dad," she said. "You look too young. This picture is at least 10 years old." I took a second look. Surely she was wrong. I looked exactly as I do now. No matter that the shirt I was wearing in the photo had been in the rag bag for the past decade.

This column is called Single Over Thirty, but I'll bet real people in their thirties think they're too young whereas people in their forties and beyond feel very much at home.

When you think about it, this ten-years-younger mind-set is really a shame. You walk around town and everyone thinks you look ten years older than you think you do. Everyone, that is, except your parents. They still think you're 17.

Internet Romance

I **think it's a great idea** to meet people on the Internet and marry them.

Yes I watch the TV evening news and I've heard the horror stories about pedophiles stalking children on the Internet. And I'm sure there have been murders, assaults, robberies, frauds and other misadventures at the hands of weird Internet chat-room people. (And at the hands of people in virtually every other setting, for that matter.)

And, yeah, yeah, I recognize that you don't know anything about people you meet in a chat room. They just sit somewhere in the world and write the words that appear electronically on your computer screen. They could be lying about everything they say. Who are they really? Are those their real names? Just how much do they misrepresent themselves? They're strangers — real strangers. The two of you have no friends in common. You don't even know anyone who knows their families, assuming people like that have families. They come at you raw, untested, and unreliable from cyberspace — wherever *that* is.

Yeah, better to keep going to the biker bar to meet people. It's a much safer environment.

I don't actually know anyone personally who has had a bad

romantic experience on the Internet. But I know two women who have married people they met there.

The first, Lilly, a woman in her early 30s, met Jerry, a few years older, in a chat room, which led to phone calls, which led to a meeting at a safe, neutral location. Sparks flew. And that ultimately led to an outdoor marriage ceremony last summer on the grounds of a sprawling municipal garden in the Midwest.

The second, fifty-ish Tommie became great friends with Paul on the Internet. They talked on the phone a few times, but she lived in Florida and he lived in Minnesota. So, as she tells it, she didn't expect to actually meet him. "Then," she said, "one day as I was cleaning the house and looked a mess, the doorbell rang."

She opened the door and a very pleasant looking man said, "Hi, I'm Paul." He had been attending a conference in a neighboring city and decided to stop by, unannounced. He never left... because she wouldn't let him.

I don't know about you, but I'm touched by both of those stories. What they have in common is that they already knew each other by the time they met. Some weeks before the ceremony, Lilly told me that Jerry "is such a genuinely nice guy," something she said she would have never known had she met him at a dance or a bar. Jerry told me that, since he met Lilly, his single friends have developed a sudden interest in the Internet.

Two final thoughts: (1.) The process of converting strangers into intimates is tricky no matter where you meet them. There are good and bad people everywhere, and (2.) Don't believe everything you read in the media. They can change their minds. The Washington Post, which has recently developed a huge financial interest in retail sales over the Internet, has decided it's a pretty safe medium after all.

Women on the Beach

This is about a woman from Europe who denigrates topless beaches because there are too many women there who ought to cover up — both for health reasons (harmful UV rays) and because they're ugly. (Her word, not mine.)

I don't see the difference between European beaches and those here in the United States. There are beautifuls and plains on both. I thought Norman Rockwell did us all a great favor by showing the beauty of ordinary people. Faces that have lived life and gained character — and perhaps an extra chin or two.

The same has got to be true of virtually every place, not just beaches. How about the last time you were in a crowded elevator? Did you look around? If so, you surely saw a variety of people, beautiful in their diversity. Some handsome, some beautiful, most heavy, dowdy and shop worn. Yet nobody has ever suggested that those of us who aren't magazine cover material should get out and take the stairs. The beauties should be glad we're there. They owe us a debt of gratitude. We're the ones who make them look beautiful. They're only young and beautiful and handsome because we make them look that way by comparison.

What kind of a world would it be if every woman looked like a movie star? Try to picture Rehoboth Beach, for instance, populated by women all of whom looked exactly like Michelle Pfeiffer — thousands of them, sprawled out on beach blankets in their skimpy little bikinis for as far as the eye could see. Little beads of perspiration forming on their long tapered legs, flat toned stomachs, tiny waists, smooth flawless skin. Picture it. Please.

Where was I? Oh yeah, well maybe that's not the best illustration.

It's like volleyball. All the accolades go to the tall players in the front row who spike the ball and get the points. But behind them are less-heralded players with incredible hands. Making split-second decisions, they place the ball in precisely the right place so one of their tall front-row team mates can spike it for the winning point, the crowd's applause, and their photos on the cover of Sports Illustrated.

The European woman's second objection was the danger of ultra violet rays. I really take exception to that. We men have been going topless for hundreds of years. More. And she doesn't even mention us. Humph, I suppose it's okay if we get an overdose of rays.

UV rays present a real danger and sun bathers should take precautions regardless of gender or how much cloth they're wearing above the waist.

I couldn't help noticing that the woman didn't mention men on the beach, ugly or not. In fact, I never hear anyone discuss men on the beach. And I have to admit, when I come back from the beach, I remember the women I've seen, but none of the men. To remember the men is like remembering the empty stretches of sand between beach blankets. You know they're there, but they don't exactly stick with you.

I had always assumed my attention exclusively to women on the beach was because I am a man. But a woman friend explained it to me by saying it's not just a man's perspective. She said a woman's form is inherently beautiful in contour, texture and grace. A woman's form is one of nature's delights, like a flower or a sunset. "Men, on the other hand," she said, "are more utilitarian. Like a Jeep."

Women Asking for a Date

My **pal Muldoon loves** to be asked out by women he likes. And he's very uncomfortable being asked out by women he doesn't particularly fancy.

No surprises there. But he actually goes out with both because he doesn't know how to say no. In fact, I suspect most men don't know how to say no with anything that approaches grace. What they know how to do (that women don't) is survive rejection relatively unscathed.

It's not a question of having some sort of gender specific talent. It's practice. Men know how to survive being rejection and/or minimize its effects because most have been enduring it since their teens. They may hate it, but, let's face it, they're good at it. Expert, in fact. They know how to make a rejected invitation sound as if it wasn't really an invitation after all. They plan their strategy and size up their chances of success beforehand. They do their homework. They concentrate on women who they know will, if not interested, let them down softly. They ask at a time when — and in a location where — they know they won't be overheard by third parties. They plan modest first dates. They're cautious, judicious, methodical. Sneaky even.

Women on the other hand haven't a clue about the agonies of such abject rejection. Sometimes, I suspect, encouraged by the feminist movement and the new freedoms, they recognize the futility of sitting at home helplessly waiting for the phone to ring. So they take the initiative. And that's when they can get blindsided by a triple whammy.

First, men typically don't know how to decline an invitation with the ease and refinement that pours forth so easily from women. By comparison, the male declination is likely to be oafish, even stupid and often down right unbelievable.

Second, some men (not Muldoon and me) misinterpret the invitation as a proposition, i.e., "She wants me." Men are accustomed to pursuing prospects themselves and may over-react when they see themselves as the quarry.

And third, men may say "yes," even though they don't want to go out. That means the woman gets to spend the whole evening with someone who doesn't want to be there.

On the other hand, women, who tend to be nurturers to start with, are experts at letting one down gently. Most women, that is. There are exceptions. Most, though, are every bit as practiced at responding to invitations as men are to issuing them. And every bit as expert.

As with men, I'm sure women like to be asked out by people they like and are uncomfortable with those they don't. But the similarity ends there. Women have told me that they virtually never go out with someone they don't want to be with. Yet their refusal is a work of art. They are smooth and they are elegant. They can say "hit the bricks" so exquisitely, so diplomatically, and with such charm and refinement that one is almost grateful afterwards.

Generally, women-initiated first dates can be difficult and awkward. But there are times when role reversal can be a piece of cake. If a couple has been dating with some regularity, it's rather nice — and risk-free — for the woman to ask the man. He'll almost always say yes and his rare balks will be for good and plausible reason. Also, if it's an appropriate special event, women should be able to ask men they know well — regardless of whether they've ever dated. It's probably best not to call it a date, though, until one is sure of the other's perspective.

It's nice to have an aspect of men/women differences that can be attributed to something other than the mysterious lining up of chromosomes, physiology, brain wiring and DNA. Still, this kind of role reversal is complicated. When the date has been made, what conventions prevail? Who picks up whom? Or do they meet on neutral ground? Who pays? Who asks for the second date?

And if nobody does, who has rejected whom?

Happy Birthday

I **have a single friend** who is dreading her upcoming 50th birthday.

She also dreaded her 40th. And she'd rather not think about someday becoming 60. Any age beyond 20 that ends with a zero, she has dreaded. I'd like to be around when she turns 100 just to see how she deals with two zeros.

Think about it: Age is a concept we've invented that enables us to keep track of who's old enough to apply for a drivers' license, vote, or receive a social security check. I can't think of any other real value to it. It's a poor predictor of one's physical condition or one's potential life span. Just looking is more reliable. Some people live to be older than 100 and others die young, so it can't be an accurate measure of one's life span. And if you've looked around at your most recent high school reunion, you know chronological age is no indication of physical condition either.

Having said all that, I have to admit that I harbor some archaic notions about age. I think providence is paying me back for my narrow view of age when I was a kid. I remember a girl in my eighth grade class who, having seen me walking with my father, said that Dad was a handsome man. "That can't be so," I answered. "My father is 35 years old."

228. - Single Over Thirty

By the time I was 35, of course, that age had been transformed into the blush of youth. And as time goes on, advanced ages become less and less daunting. Today, I have new heroes - people who have retained their youthful vigor at rather advanced ages.

Al Hirshfield, the cartoonist whose show-biz caricatures appear in the New York Times, is 98 and still puts in a regular work day. In a recent interview he said he doesn't think much about his age until someone mentions it to him.

I want to be like him.

Mike Wallace of 60 Minutes just celebrated his 83rd birthday. At a Press Club luncheon when he was a youthful 78, someone asked him how much longer he intended to go on working. "I plan to retire when I'm 80," he said. There's that pesky age ending with a zero, again. To his credit, he's still unretired at age 85.

I saw him on a TV talk show recently with Pulitzer Prize winning author Studs Terkel who was born the year the Titanic sank. He's 90.

Birthdays shouldn't be about age but rather a celebration of one's appearance on this earth; of all the lives one has enriched over the years; of the love one's given and received; of one's progeny; of one's accomplishments; one's unique talents, and one's contributions to the lives of others.

It should be a celebration, not a lament.

One should celebrate one's birthday the way we celebrate George Washington's. No one keeps track of his age (He turned 269 this year). People still pass around his picture on one-dollar bills as he looked when he was 50. Abe

Lincoln, who is only 192, appears as a 50-something-year-old on five dollar bills.

Incidentally, my single friend who is turning 50 looks eternally young and brings new youth, vigor, and pizzazz to the decade of the 50s.

But I doubt that she sees it that way.

It's ***All*** ***Been a*** **Lesson** ***to Me***

---

*Mystical Messages * Don't Take It Personally * How Life Is * How Life Isn't * The Great Communicator * Thornden Parkish Feelings * Pain and Suffering * Small Potatoes * Work * Real Women Don't Spit * Relationship Round*

Mystical Messages

A **date, as everyone knows,** is a social engagement between two people with some potential for an eventual romantic connection.

A couple that has dated once, however, cannot be said to be dating, because "dating" (also called "seeing" someone) means they have had a semi-exclusive series of dates, suggesting some on-going romantic interest in each other. Generally one uses the alternate term "seeing someone" and its sister term "involved" to subtly avoid revealing the other partner's name. All three refer to a semi-exclusive relationship.

Everybody knows that.

But semi-exclusive isn't the same as exclusive. And just because he/she is dating you doesn't mean he/she isn't also dating someone else.

Not everyone knows that.

If the relationship is truly exclusive it's called "going with." Or better yet the slightly archaic "going steady."

And, whereas a smooth-talking outsider might conceivably pry apart a couple who are merely "dating," he or she would have his or her work cut out trying to come between a couple who were "going together." And "going steady," out-dated though the term may be, still delivers an unmistakable message. And a warning: i.e. Don't even think about flirting. Eyes forward. Let the rest of the world go by. It has nothing to do with you and your sweetie.

It's all very confusing, but it makes one wonder about some of the other mystical messages of relationships. Some friends and I tried to sort-out all of this the other day and decided some definitions are in order:

Sort of Dating — A dating relationship that is about to change because at least one partner is in conflict. If someone says they are "sort of dating," think of it as a storm warning for them and possibly an opportunity for you.

A BTN Date — Sometimes one must settle for a BTN date (Better Than Nothing). My friend Orme was certain opportunity was knocking when he learned Tanya was seeing a BTN date. Imagine his disappointment when it turned out the guy was also a BTO date (Better Than Orme).

Went With -- Past tense of "Going With."

Still Friends — A misnomer. They're not really friends. They've just entered into a non-aggression pact. They are past lovers who no longer do things together, but they've agreed to be civil and not bad-mouth each other in front of mutual friends.

Shacking Up — A remnant from a bye-gone era when it was considered promiscuous for an unmarried couple to live together.

An Item — A couple rumored to be in the throes of developing a romantic relationship.

Smitten — Struck by one of the fat baby's wobbly arrows.

Has the Hots For: — Similar to "Smitten" with a little less romance and a bit more libido.

And, of course, these mystical messages are not always verbal. To wit:

Kiss — A smacking of the lips against those of one who is lip-smacking back.

Sucking Face — A tongue mingling, out-of-control kiss that usually gratifies participants and embarrasses everybody else.

Peck — A quick, perfunctory kiss.

A Kiss on the Cheek — A friendly, no-promises-made gesture of affection.

A Kiss on the Neck — This kiss normally comes just as a man and a woman are disengaging from a hug. It's an afterthought, typically by just one of the huggers. It's lovely to receive. The recipient feels valued. This kiss is innocent and not to be confused with...

A Hickey — A reddish bite, suck or nibble mark left on the neck or trapezius by an impassioned, zealous lover at a moment of heightened sexual activity. It goes away eventually, but not before some snickering clown in your office notices it publicly and in full voice.

Ear Nibble — It's seldom that the nibbler and the nibblee both groove on this activity. But it happens. Hopefully, not in public.

Don't Take It Personally

A**t a discussion meeting** a few years ago, a woman calmly explained how she is never hurt — barely even affected — when a man turns her down.

"I know all men have their preferences, types of women who turn them on and types who don't," she said. "I am the turn-on type for some men and not for others. I know that. When a man shows no interest, I don't take it personally. It has a lot more to do with him and his preferences than with me. Besides," she said, "I have preferences of my own."

Such wisdom. Such maturity. Such self control. I'm impressed. In fact, I'm so impressed that I'm almost embarrassed to admit that I'm highly skeptical of anyone's ability to handle such subjective matters with such objectivity. When she made that declaration, oohs and aahs came from the group. I assumed we all knew we shouldn't take such affronts personally. But actually not being hurt by them is something else. To me, her claimed ability to not be affected was nothing short of superhuman.

"Don't take it personally" is the kind of advice one might expect to hear from a robed white-haired guru sitting cross-legged in front of a cave high in the Himalayas. Once back to real life in the lowlands it can be hard advice to follow.

There was a scene in the movie Lawrence of Arabia in which Lawrence held the flat of his hand just above a lit candle. One of his cohorts said, "He's got this trick where he doesn't feel the pain." To which Lawrence replied, "the trick isn't to not feel the pain, it's to feel it and not mind."

I put the Three-Plus lady in Lawrence's league in her ability to get her mind to do her bidding.

Okay, Lawrence and the lady are extremes. So what are the things one takes personally that one ought not to? I think it would be nice to not take rejection — of any kind — personally.

Here are three test scenarios. How would you respond?

1. They gave someone else the job you applied for.

a. That's okay. They must have thought the other person fit the job description better.

b. I should have presented my qualifications better.

c. They don't like me. I'm a loser. I'll never get a job.

2. Your significant other suddenly recognizes that he/she is a free spirit and splits.

a. What a jerk.

b. A leopard can't change its spots. People are what they are. It has nothing to do with me personally.

c. Why can't I sustain a relationship? I'll make concessions. Maybe that'll bring him/her back.

3. Your friends left the ball game without you. So you had to take the bus.

a. These people are not my friends.

b. Wait till they realize they forgot me. They'll be so embarrassed.

c. They just forgot. Everyone forgets. It's part of the human condition.

Someone who doesn't take things personally would surely find the choices as simple as abc.

How Life is...

I don't know how life is for everybody. But I do know how it seemed to some pretty famous people throughout the ages.

About a decade ago, I compiled more than 100 quotes from mostly famous people who attempted to describe life in a single sentence or two. It turned out to be a very insightful exercise and great fun. Here's a sample:

My life is like a stroll on the beach,

As near to the ocean's edge as I can go.

— **Thoreau** 1817-1862

What life turns out to be is all coming attractions and no movie.

— **Mort Saul** (1927-)

Life shrinks or expands in proportion to one's courage.

— **Anais Nin** (1903-1977)

Don't tell me life isn't a Shakespearean tragedy.

240. - Single Over Thirty

— Charlie Brown's sister to Charlie Brown after dropping her marble fudge ice cream cone on the sidewalk; in the July 3, 1987 Peanuts cartoon by **Charles M. Schultz**

Look at the words in a new way. "Row, row, row your boat" ... your own destiny, your equipment in life ... "gently" not hurriedly ... "down the stream" of life ... "merrily," always positive ... "life is but a dream" ... life is something you make up as you go along, something you want, anything you want it to be.

— Fire-walker **Joyce Quick** who had her workshop students sing, "Row, row, row your boat," just before leading them barefoot across 1,300-degree coals. (Washington Post, Page Bl, Dec. 18, 1984.)

My life is one demd horrid grind.

— From Nicholas Nickelby by **Charles Dickens** (1812-1870)

Life isn't all beer and skittles.

— **Thomas Hughes** (1822-1896)

This is the true joy of life, the being used for a purpose recognized by yourself as a mighty one; the being thoroughly worn out before you are thrown on the scrap heap; the being a force of Nature instead of a feverish selfish little clod of ailments and grievances complaining that the world will not devote itself to making you happy.

— **George Bernard Shaw,** (1856-1950) Man and Superman (1903) Epistle Dedicatory

Life is not a spectacle or a feast, it is a predicament.

— **George Santayana** (1863-1952)

Life is an experiment.

— **Oliver Wendall Holmes, Jr.** (1841-1935) (in 1919)

Life is the thing you have before you die.

— "The World According to Garp," author **John Irving** (1942-) paraphrased from Garp's mother's words to him after his grandfather's burial.

It took me a long time to understand that misfortune — loneliness, sickness, financial reverses, malicious gossip, shabby treatment by friends, problems with children, the untimely death of family and friends, the duplicity of lovers — is a permanent part of life and should be expected to continue with varying degrees of severity as long as one lives... The difference (between people) is the way in which they tackle what life sets before them.

— 78-year-old **Mortimer Levitt,** custom-shirt mogul, in a Parade Magazine article,"How To Be Classy In Spite of Yourself" (May 12, 1985)

Some people march in the parade of life, some people stand on the curb and watch, and others don't even know the damn thing's going on.

— **Anonymous**

Life is what happens while we're making other plans.

— **John Lennon** (1940-1980)

Life would be a lot simpler if we didn't have bodies.

— **Anne Goldbaum,** in a discussion of the ectoplane. (1985)

Birth and copulation, and death.

242. - Single Over Thirty

That's all the facts when you come to brass tacks.

— **T.S. Eliot,** (1888-1930) Sweeney Agonistes (unfinished, pub. 1932)

Life can only be understood backwards; but it must be lived forwards.

— "Bloom County" cartoonist **Berke Breathed,** (1957-) (in cartoon appearing April 24, 1988)

And finally, from my daughter's refrigerator door this list entitled, Rules for Being Human:

1. You will receive a body. You may like it or hate it, but it will be yours for the entire period.

2. You will learn lessons. You are enrolled in a full-time, informal school called life. You may like the lessons or think them irrelevant and stupid.

3. There are no mistakes, only lessons.

4. A lesson is repeated until it is learned.

5. Learning lessons does not end.

6. "There" is no better than "here."

7. Others are mirrors of you.

8. What you make of your life is up to you.

9. Your answers lie inside you.

10. You will forget all this.

-- **Anonymous**

How Life Isn't

P**oor Sophie. Life doesn't** make much sense to her because when she was a child her parents were seldom home, so she had to learn about love, life and sex from the movies. How sad.

It's sad because movies are not about how life is, they're about how life isn't. For instance:

— In the movies, the courtship is fraught with difficulties, then they get married and live happily ever after. (Sophie's courtship was a breeze, but her marriage was Armageddon.)

— Movie women always have shaved legs and under-arms, even in caveman movies. (Sophie wonders exactly when the safety razor was invented.)

— Movie women wear make-up to bed and awaken with it still intact. (When Sophie tried it, she ruined her pillow case and got eye shadow in her ear.)

— A typical movie woman never thinks to conk the bad guy who is fighting with her love-interest — or to run out of harm's way. Instead she stands there wide-eyed, hand to mouth. In those rare cases when she does conk the bad guy, she misses and knocks out the good guy instead. (Sophie has faultless aim and an aggressive nature.)

— Movie detectives are out-of shape, portly, middle-aged men who drink hard and chain smoke. Yet, dressed in suits and ties, they can chase the bad guys down the street, over fences, through traffic, up the steps to the elevated train station, across the platform, down the other side, up a water tower, through a warehouse and on and on without getting winded. (In real life, they'd shout "you'll get your summons in the mail," without taking a step.)

— In the movies, high-powered women executives wear mini skirts and five-inch heels to work. (By contrast, for the first six weeks, Sophie thought her new boss was a man.)

— Movie women don't need to go to the bathroom when they first wake up, but shower at every opportunity. (Going to the bathroom has been every day's first activity for as long as Sophie can remember.)

— Movie suitcases are weightless. (Sophie's need wheels.)

— Movie people speaking on the phone neither identify themselves nor say goodbye. (Nobody recognizes Sophie's phone voice and, if she didn't say goodbye, they'd call her right back.)

— Movie beds have special L-shaped sheets that come up to arm pit level on women but only to the waist on men. (Neither Bloomingdale's nor Macy's carries them.)

— No one ever needs a Kleenex after sex in the movies. (Sophie's is never out of reach.)

— All movie women moan during sex, but none sweats. (Sophie sweats, but doesn't moan for fear of waking the kids — or, on a really memorable night, the whole neighborhood.)

— Two total strangers, upon falling into bed together, always reach an incredibly intense, mutual and simultaneous orgasm on the first try. (Sophie is still waiting.)

— Movie characters hear the most important part of the TV news broadcast the moment they turn on the set. They turn it off before hearing other details. (First Sophie gets a Viagra commercial, then the weather, and finally sports. She already missed the lead news story.)

— When movie people immerge from cabs, they always have the exact change. (Sophie needs to break a 20.)

— Movie people never have to wait for cabs, trains, buses or airplanes. (The only time Sophie's transportation is on time is when she's late.)

— Movie drivers never have to shift gears or signal, and can spend long periods talking to their passengers without looking at the road. (Sophie lives because she never tried it.)

— Movie cars always park right in front and are never locked. (Sophie has to find a public parking garage, then walk three blocks. She has religiously locked her new car ever since her old one was stolen.)

And finally, my personal favorite: The ugliest, most foul, most unkempt, dirtiest, sloppiest, hygiene-deficient, low-life appears on screen. He's spent his life living in a cave with wild animals. His face is scarred and caked; hair grows out his ears and his nose, and more hair creeps up the back of his grimy neck like two giant angora caterpillars. Nevertheless, each time he sneers, he shows the whitest, most even, most gleaming, pristine, orthodontically perfect, teeth you've ever seen. Well! He may not be every woman's dream date, but apparently he brushes after every meal, flosses regularly, and sees his dentist at least twice a year.

Everything that happens in movies is designed to fit either the plot, the budget, or the pace of the film. Imitating real life is not in the mix.

But implausibility often is.

I watched a movie on TV the other night in which Michelle Pfeiffer and Jack Nicholson fall in love in a single afternoon. He's an unemployed, vengeful, over-aged editor who's losing his hair. She's a young, knock-em-dead beautiful, self-absorbed heiress with an attitude. She tells him he's boring and he says she's spoiled and obnoxious. A match made in Heaven.

Oh, and did I mention, he's also a werewolf.

I wonder what Sophie would have learned from that.

The Great Communicator

Quiz: **What human faculty** can communicate across cultural lines all over the globe?

Hint: It's can also make people fall in love. Or not.

Further hint: It is alternately washed, painted, packed in mud, veiled, massaged, powdered, surgically enhanced, ogled, averted, slapped, and kissed. And the one owned by Helen of Troy is said to have launched a thousand ships.

Answer: It's the principle instrument of recognition among humans and, hands down, the sexiest part of the human body. It's the face and it tells volumes about you whether you want it to or not.

It tells your age, your gender, your race, your disposition, your mood, your health, and a whole lot more.

All the creatures on earth have faces, but for sheer medley of expression, they pale by comparison to ours. We are recognized by our faces. It's a better ID than a social security number. And we recognize others by theirs -- even long-dead people we've never met like George Washington, Abraham Lincoln and Mona Lisa. Faces are endlessly varied and immediately recognizable to us.

Not so with other members of the animal kingdom. It has always puzzled me, for instance, how baby calves can find their mothers (or their mothers find them) when they get separated in a herd of several thousand head of Herefords stretching to the horizon. Certainly they don't examine every other cow's face or call out to each other.

Maybe cows recognize the calf's distressed mooing. From my viewpoint, one baby cow is the same as another. I'd advise the mama cow to just pick up the closest look-alike. But I don't suppose she'd see it that way. Anyway, this is about human faces, not cows.

In my view, the face is also the sexiest part of the human body because it displays so much intimate information about the wearer. You may disagree in favor of parts of the anatomy that are kept under wrap. And British satirist Lady Mary Wortly Montague might have agreed with you. Two hundred years ago, she caused a stir when she wrote "If it were the fashion to go naked, people's faces would hardly be noticed." Anthropologists have been gleefully disagreeing with her ever since. Me too.

Facial recognition among our species is a big deal. Think of what it would be like if we didn't recognize each other so easily and immediately. Movie stars wouldn't be famous. Paper money could have anyone's face on bills. Making friends would be difficult. Portrait painters would starve. And there'd be no "wanted" posters in the Post Office. The list is endless.

In a TV drama some years ago, Jack Benny played a character with the world's most forgettable face, a circumstance that wreaked havoc with his personal life -- until he discovered he could rob banks with impunity because no witnesses could remember what he looked like.

There's a lot to be said for having a good looking face --

although I'm not sure how "good looking" is defined. Tight skin, high cheekbones, clear complexion, pleasant expression would probably be a good start. Except sometimes. It's even difficult to tell what makes a person homely. There is a unique modeling agency in New York that specializes in ugly models. I saw a composite of their faces and thought they were more interesting than ugly -- except the man who could throw his lower lip up over his nose. He was ugly.

The most incredible ability of the human face is the information it can project: And so easily. Unlike spoken language, even without instruction virtually anyone from any culture can express anger, joy, cynicism, suspicion, mistrust, smugness, surprise, sympathy and fatigue. They can twinkle, scowl, beam, reject, affirm, disdain, threaten, beguile, question, tease and pout. It's possible to talk so much, one gets hoarse. But have you ever heard anyone complain that his/her face is tired? I don't think so.

In the 1974 movie, "Airport" the role of a diabolical little old lady in her 70s earned Helen Hayes an Oscar using little more than her face. By her fleeting facial expressions, she told movie-goers everything she was thinking -- so subtly, yet so unmistakably -- often without uttering a word. Helen Hayes and most accomplished actors make a very good living by skillfully manipulating their faces to fit the script.

For those non-actors among us, the face can be a bit of a tattle tale, exposing some very personal information. A few years ago, I got word over the weekend that my father had suffered a stroke. The moment I stepped into the office on Monday morning, several people asked me what was wrong. How did they know? They read a signal I didn't know I was broadcasting.

On a happier note, there's a Viagra commercial that makes

much the same point when a guy named Joe shows up for work with a twinkle in his eye.

Thornden Parkish Feelings

Long before relationship lists were in vogue, Dean Charles C. Noble of Syracuse University (my alma mater) listed seven qualities a couple should have going for itself to make a relationship work permanently, assuming both parties were honest and respectable. (I suppose that means this doesn't necessarily work for thieves and other low-lifes.)

1. Good health.

2. Religious similarity.

3. Thornden Parkish feelings.

4. Financial stability.

5. Similarities of outside interests

6. Be buddies

7. Psychological maturity

I'd like to revisit them now that I've had experience as a single person, a married person, a parent, and then a single person again. So here it is: Yesterday's advice analyzed in today's light:

252. - Single Over Thirty

1. Good health. One doesn't always have a choice after the relationship has hit high gear. Deserting one who is ill is a no-no. Bad form. However, beginning a relationship with someone who is in poor health can be an iffy proposition. And if you're the one who is in poor health, you may not be moved easily by moonlight and roses anyway.

2. Religious similarity. Probably less important today than it was when I was in school. It also has to depend upon the ardor with which one holds and practices one's religious convictions. A non-practicing Protestant and a lax Catholic, for instance, may have a shot at it.

3. Thornden Parkish feelings. You had to be there to understand. Thorndon Park was a richly beautiful public garden on a hillside just off campus and perpetually peopled by handsome young men and beautiful coeds. At the top of the hill was a secluded water tower with a panoramic view of the garden and the campus beyond; a great place for lovers. The dean's point was: if you have no desire to go there, you probably wouldn't be happy in that particular relationship. Some things don't change.

4. Financial stability. At least one of you ought to have a job. Nowadays, probably both.

5. Similarity of interests. Note he said "similarity' not "exact match." If one hates the activities the other loves, it could spell trouble.

6. Be buddies. Be a pal. Laugh together. Have little adventures together. Confidences. I doubt that has changed.

7. Psychological maturity. My guess all these years later is that he meant, simply, "grow up." Don't be petty, jealous, selfish, angry, spiteful, irresponsible, stingy, moody, secretive, insensitive, critical or aloof.

Pain and Suffering

Start with this premise: Pain is good for you.

It bolsters your resolve and teaches you not to make the same mistake twice. Suffering, on the other hand, is one of those human functions that drags one down and serves no purpose — like worrying.

I knew a woman once who was so into suffering that I assumed she was playing the tragic, martyred, long-suffering heroine of her own internal playlet. I, on the other hand, hated suffering and went to great extremes to avoid it. I still do.

As I got to know her better, I found she didn't actually like to suffer, it was just that she thought that was what she was supposed to do when she was hurt or endured a loss. She felt that failure to visibly suffer trivialized the loss. For her, melancholy and displays of bleak emotion were part of the process. The more she suffered, the more virtuous she felt — like those toothless old women from some Mediterranean countries who, draped in black hooded garb, weep and wail at public funerals — even though they didn't necessarily know the deceased.

When she broke things off with her boyfriend, she was

upset that he seemed to suffer more than she did. "He out-suffered me," she told me. Bummer. This was one contest, I would want to lose.

The Lamoureaux kids of my childhood disdained mercurochrome in favor of methylate for cuts and scrapes. They said mercurochrome was no good because it didn't hurt. Methylate, on the other hand, burned like fire, a sure sign it was working.

I chose mercurochrome.

My daughter has a computer that locks up every time it gets to the \oldtime\download directory. She can't read the directory, or erase it, or look at it. The computer just freezes there. Nothing on the keyboard works. The mouse buttons have no effect. But the little red light on the CPU keeps blinking away, showing the computer is churning as hard as it can... and accomplishing nothing. It's hung up.

I know people like that. They get hung up on some bit of pain — usually the breakup of a marriage or relationship — and they hang there, using emotional energy just like the computer. But, unlike the computer, they can stop being a victim and get on with things like life and fun and the future.

Most of the time, pain is fleeting with only the memory lingering on — hopefully to help you avoid future mistakes. It shows you what you ought not to keep doing. But if you want it to be some sort of unfair punishment, it can become that too.

A friend was telling me about ways people she knows deal with pain. One eats too much, exercises too little and gains weight. "But it's all right," she said, "that's her way with dealing with the pain." Another smokes. "Bad for his health, but it's a trade-off — it helps him deal with the pain." Another deals with pain by excessive activity.

Sometimes, though, physical and emotional pain doesn't go away. It lingers. Then one has to live with it. A woman friend with a serious congenital problem once asked me if I ever wondered if other people were in more, less, or the same level of pain as I was. I was startled. "I'm not in pain," I said incredulously. It never occurred to me that people lived all their lives in pain. Apparently, it had never occurred to her that they didn't.

Certain magnificent people successfully function through it — people like Bill Cosby, Stephen Hawkins, Christopher Reeve, and Birdie Kocher.

What? You've never heard of Birdie Kocher? Sixty-pound Birdie Kocher, an old woman who lived on the farm next to ours when I was a child, had painful arthritis for as long as anyone could remember. But the first time she mentioned it was when she moved to a nursing home where they gave her pain killers. She said it was the first time she could remember not being in pain.

My point is that suffering is something one often has some control over, whereas pain is an inevitable part of the human experience that serves an important function.

On the downside, of course, pain hurts. And everybody except a few weird people, don't much care for that.

Small Potatoes

The most difficult self-improvement chore, a self-help guru once told me, is deciding what to improve. Once identified, it's a relative piece of cake to correct a fault, he said.

His point, I think, was that it's not easy to see yourself objectively. And therefore, it's difficult to recognize your shortcomings.

I know what I need to correct and it's no piece of cake. It's my penchant for getting bogged down in irritating trifles that I can't do anything about anyway.

Here's an example: When I take the Metro to work, it's crowded — especially at Metro Center where I get off. And invariably people stand in the doorway like corrosion in a water pipe forcing a slow flow of passengers into and out of the Metro car.

That bothers me. But what bothers me more is the fact that it bothers me at all. In the range of world events, the congestion at one door to one car at one stop in one city's rapid transportation system is small potatoes. And I want to not notice, not care and above all not clutter my thoughts with such small stuff. I want to dismiss it like flicking a fly off my shirt sleeve. Barely noticed and immediately forgotten.

When I have time to ruminate I want to try to solve life's little puzzles. Cook-up ways to streamline my business. Put some creative thought into composing my Christmas list. Remember pleasant experiences. Plan my weekend. Make decisions. I want my private thoughts to be cheerful and to count for something.

Instead, I agitate over three heavy women with huge flopping pocketbooks who, moving slowly and three-abreast, block my way through narrow corridors. I am provoked by the healthy young guy who pushes the down button on the elevator, then decides to walk down the steps after all — leaving the rest of us to wait for the empty elevator to go down to the lower level then back up again before we can use it.

And while my mind is so occupied, favorite issues go unanalyzed; plans remain incomplete; and sometimes promising thoughts are fragmented by trivia.

Granted, the world hardly suffers when I dwell too much on small potatoes. But that's not the point. The larger issue here is how large one's world is. And I want mine to be too big to be sidetracked every time two klutzes block a Metro doorway.

Work

A change of work is as good as a rest." That's what my grandfather used to say.

He was wrong.

Rest is the opposite of work. So how can a change of work be as good as a rest? It can't. I knew that all along. My grandfather was in his sixties, owned the farm I spent my summers on, was president of the Plymouth National Bank, and was the consummate "boss." I, on the other hand, was six-going-on-seven, a soon-to-be second grader, and I owned a yo-yo, a bottle cap and three smooth pebbles. It didn't seem politic at the time to pit my opinion against his.

But experience told me that stopping weeding a row of potatoes that was so long it disappeared over the horizon, then going straight to digging dandelions out of my grandmother's sprawling lawn was not restful.

Remembering his words got me to thinking about work and play — and the difference between the two. Work, it always seemed to me, was the stuff you had to do that was so unpleasant they had to pay you to do it. You didn't want to work and they didn't want to pay you. But you needed money and they needed a job done. So you worked and they paid.

Play, however, was something one did for free. The rewards were that it was fun, could be stopped at any time, that it required no real commitment. And if you did it right, it could be stimulating, creative and uplifting.

But it's just not that simple. If you're having fun while you're working, is it still work? The answer has to be yes, if you're still getting paid. If you're suddenly not being paid anymore, you might find the fun has been replaced by panic.

Conversely, if you make a living doing something others do for fun, is it work? Yes it is. And chances are if you are getting paid to do something most people do for fun, you bring some incredible skills to the process and you are getting paid very well.

In announcing his retirement, Redskins fullback John Riggins told an interviewer he had never really worked. He played. First high school football, then college, then pro. Now for the first time, he faced the prospect of the other kind of work. My guess is that having been paid so well to play for all those years, he faced his prospects rather calmly.

There are other advantages of work besides money, of course: the structure it gives to one's days, the skills it builds, the contribution it makes to the common good, and the ability it gives one to be financially secure.

But not everyone sees it that way — like the bum who was admonished by a lady to get a job.

"Why?," he asked.

"So you can earn money," she replied.

"Why?"

"So you can build a financial nest egg."

"Why?"

"So you won't have to work when you get old."

"But I'm not working now."

Real Women Don't Spit

I **have only seen a woman** spit once. And that was when I was in high school. One of those burley women who operated the stitching machines at the local ladies garment factory erupted from the shop one day and fouled the sidewalk just as I walked by. And it was so disgusting, I still remember it all these years later.

There seems to be a self-imposed double standard here. Real women don't spit. Yet, men have been chewing tobacco and spitting out black, disgusting slime in public for more than a century. Traditional bar rooms had several spittoons to keep that stuff off the floor. Major league baseball players -- especially pitchers -- spit at will before TV audiences numbering in the millions. And do you really think NFL football players need all that time in huddles just to discuss plays?

Hey, we men may be biologically compelled to spit.

But that doesn't mean we're not sensitive. Some of us. If women only knew the machinations we go through to spit in ways that are undetectable by women.

Have you ever seen a frog shoot its tongue out to catch a insect in mid air... then swallow it whole? Now that's what I call disgusting. Let's keep things in perspective. We men don't do that.

What is needed here is not to rag on men about a quintessentially male compulsion, but rather to suggest some refinements of technique for those spit-obsessive men to aspire to.

There are several perfectly acceptable, albeit subterfugel, ways one can deftly rid oneself of the offending yuck that builds up in one's throat lending an unwanted gargling sound to one's diction.

But the methods require a certain amount of caution, initiative and skill. Let's say you just got over a cold and are still experiencing some post-nasal drip. You go out on a date and everything is going along swimmingly except for one thing: You need to get rid of that stuff that's accumulating in the back of your throat.

Obviously, the best place to get rid of it is in the restroom. People there are usually absorbed by their own agendas and don't look at each other, so they probably won't even notice you. Still, restrooms are not always available.

As an acceptable alternative, you can bury your nose

in a large tissue and quietly and carefully spit into it, giving the appearance of merely wiping your nose -- which is acceptable behavior considering the alternative. But when employing this ruse, one must be exceedingly cautious. It's all too easy for the overburdened tissue to give way, depositing your spittle in your hand, on your tie, along your sleeve, atop your shoe, down your shirt, at the rim of your jacket, under your watchband, or a humiliating combination of the above.

Perhaps a better plan is to use those little moments when you are alone for just an instant. One of my favorite such twinkling is while walking around the car to open the door for my passenger. There's a magic moment after you've left their peripheral vision and before coming into view of the rear-view mirror. At that precise moment, you can let 'er rip. Three cautions, though:

(1.) Always walk around the rear of the car.

(2.) Try to time the offensive thwack sound to coincide with the closing of your car door.

(3.) Work on your spitting technique. There are few things as unromantic as arriving at the passenger's door with spittle dangling from your chin.

When you are driving alone on a deserted strip of highway, there is no reason you can't just open the window and spit to your heart's content. Just be careful that:

264. - Single Over Thirty

(1.) You're not traveling so fast that the wind blows it back to you.

(2.) You don't hit the outside rear-view mirror.

(3.) The window really is open.

A Relationship Round

Enough of this hanging out by yourself. You want a relationship.

So how are you going to go about getting one? We assume you have been out and about for awhile, but you've been sort of drifting. No real plan. Now you're going to devise a new strategy. You're focused. You're going to launch a serious pursuit. Look out everyone. Here you come.

What do you do first? Obviously you have to put your body out where appropriate people of the opposite sex congregate. You can't do it all by phone, fax and e-mail. So you go to dances, parties, clam bakes, singles excursions, pot lucks, bridge walks, discussions, wine and cheese socials, and you learn how to do the latest line dances. You get involved, throw parties at your house, join committees, volunteer your time, and help set-up for and clean-up after practically every social event in sight.

Soon it begins to pay off. You meet some people who appeal to you. So you do some one-on-one talking to get to know them better. You try to sort out the lost causes, that is, otherwise attractive prospects who are not available to anyone and very needy people who seem to be available to everyone. You do "couples" things like having candle-lit dinners for two, going for long hand-in-hand walks, seeing romantic foreign films, watching sunsets together, and walking barefoot on the beach. You narrow down the field.

This is exciting. It could be the most thrilling, wonderful thing that ever happened to you if you choose the right person. Or a disaster, if you don't. In the midst of your excitement, you can't help remembering people in you past who seemed so perfect, but turned out to be so sullied. So, to avoid making a serious mistake, you apply the lessons you learned from your marriage and your past romances. Only a fool would willfully make the same mistakes twice. Then you measure your possible partners against your own personal set of standards. Those standards include your non-negotiables, naturally. What-the-heck, why not compare Myers-Briggs scores too? You can't have too much information.

Big surprise: No one measures up. They're all flawed. They're humorless or they drink too much. Or they smoke (non-negotiable #1.) They double-dip their celery in the cheese dip. They're too young or too old. They're sloppy. Or an obsessive neatnik. Your mother would never approve.

It's all very confusing and discouraging. Could this tentative attraction you feel be purely physical? Whoa! You need some time to sort things out. There's no big rush, you know. And making the right choice is paramount. Better to be safe than sorry.

Don't let yourself be stampeded into making a serious mistake. Why not hang out for awhile? You need time to yourself — time to get re-oriented; to sort it all out. Time alone.

(Go back to line one and start over. This is after all, as the headline suggests, a round.)

After Words

*T**o sum up,** here is a sampling of the advice and (occasionally) insight hidden away in all those columns:*

1. You can't tell the content of one's character from across the dance floor — but there's a lot you can tell.

2. Don't expect too much from mere physical attraction, but don't expect anything without it.

3. If you are prone to cuss and swear, select your audience with supreme care.

4. Deliberately treat your partner as well as you routinely treat your dog.

5. Give charity cheerfully to homeless people you meet on the street where there's no middleman taking his cut and where, if you hang around, you may actually see your donation transformed into a Big Mac.

6. If extraterrestrials could see us, they'd think we have some weird rituals and constraints. And they'd be right.

7. There's a subgroup of humans that goes through life, from childhood through old age, joined at the hip with someone — anyone — of the opposite sex.

8. Don't limit your dating activities to dinner and a movie. There's a whole world out there.

9. No, Virginia, there isn't someone for everyone. But for some very nice people, there's a small army.

10. Yes, Virginia, there really is a cupid. It's you.

11. Negotiate everything — even when you think you know how it's going to turn out.

12. Don't expect real people to walk on water.

13. Don't be late — except sometimes. Don't be early — ever.

14. Listen when people tell you their shortcomings. It may not just be modesty talking.

15. Give all the people in your life a turn at being number one.

16. Beware of mere concepts posing as things that are real. Concepts have no weight, form, texture or place in time. And they're everywhere.

17. Don't expect a second marriage to be anything like the first.

18. Beware! Marriage can make you boring.

19. Most men haven't a clue about women's burdens.

20. Shopping as a form of recreation is an enigma to men; a fundamental part of life to women.

21. If you want to learn about life, read a novel, see a movie or listen to a radio drama — then expect the opposite. Fiction is about how life *isn't.* That's why it's called fiction.

22. Don't utter those three little words so indiscriminately that they lose their meaning.

23. Don't fight. Discuss instead. Fighting leaves scars.

24. When looking deeply into your partner's eyes, don't expect to see anything except your own reflection... unless you happen to be an eye doctor.

25. There really is such a thing as absolute truth. It's everywhere. But finding it is something else.

26. Don't spit into the wind.

27. Men: To live as long as women do, keep a cool head, take your vitamins, and get regular check-ups. Misplaced machismo can be fatal.

28. Be what you want your partner to be.

29. Bathtubs are too small for you; take a shower.

30. Look at interesting people when you talk to them, but don't lock eyes. Yet.

31. Essentially, singles hunt; marrieds preserve.

32. The only rule is that there are no rules.

33. Expect men to be different from women — and from each other.

34. Don't expect men to follow two conversations simultaneously. That's a gender-specific talent.

35. Luckily, men's fragile egos tend to keep their aggressions in check.

36. Nobody cares if you're not a good dancer. Just get up and dance.

37. Observe all birthdays (especially your own) as you do George Washington's. Forget about age. Celebrate the person.

38. Don't buy into the notion that a change of work is as good as a rest. It's not even close.

39. Never swear before noon.

40. Don't take anything personally if you can find another explanation.

41. *There* is no better than *here.*

42. Avoid suffering whenever possible — even when you're in pain.

43. Choose to live in a world that's too big for pettiness.

44. Expect change.

45. The process of converting strangers into intimates is risky no matter where you meet them — not just on the Internet.

46. Wear sun screen.

47. Don't belch at formal dinners. It's not likely to be seen as a compliment to the chef.

48. Don't expect wisdom from men who wear their hats in restaurants.

49. Keep your friends — even after they disappoint you.

50. Answer your e-mail messages as conscientiously as you do your phone messages.